MELROSE
Confidential

MELROSE
Confidential

**AN INSIDER'S UNAUTHORIZED GUIDE
TO HOLLYWOOD'S HOTTEST ADDRESS**

Roberta Caploe and Jamie Caploe

A CITADEL PRESS BOOK
PUBLISHED BY CAROL PUBLISHING GROUP

Interior book design by LaBreacht Design.

A Citadel Press Book
Published by Carol Publishing Group
Citadel Press is a registered trademark of Carol Communications, Inc.
Editorial Offices: 600 Madison Avenue, New York, N.Y. 10022
Sales and Distribution Offices: 120 Enterprise Avenue, Secaucus, N.J. 07094
In Canada: Canadian Manda Group, One Atlantic Avenue, Suite 105, Toronto,
Ontario M6K 3E7
Queries regarding rights and permissions should be addressed to Carol Pub-
lishing Group, 600 Madison Avenue, New York, N.Y. 10022

Carol Publishing Group books are available at special discounts for bulk pur-
chases, sales promotion, fund-raising, or educational purposes. Special edi-
tions can be created to specifications. For details, contact: Special Sales
Department, Carol Publishing Group, 120 Enterprise Avenue, Secaucus, N.J.
07094

Manufactured in the United States of America
10 9 8 7 6 5 4 3 2 1

Caploe, Roberta.
    Melrose confidential: an insider's unauthorized guide to Hollywood's
hottest address / Roberta and Jamie Caploe.
        p.   cm.
    "A Citadel Press book."
    ISBN 0-8065-1743-3
    1. Melrose Place (Television program)   I. Caploe, Jamie.
II. Title.
PN1992.77.M44C36 1996   95-26389
791.45'72—dc20   CIP

PHOTOGRAPH ACKNOWLEDGMENTS: Fox/MP & TV Archives: ii, 80, 108-
109; Lisa O'Connor/Celebrity Photo: 5, 12, 20, 40, 61, 117; Fox/Diego Uchitel/
MP & TV Archive: x, xiv; Fox/D. Fineman/MP & TV Archive: 149; Fox/Mathew
Rolston/MP & TV Archive: 84-85; Albert Ortega/Celebrity Photo: 137; Janet
Gough/Celebrity Photo: 69, 77; John Paschal/Celebrity Photo: 134, 149, 160-
161; Tammie Arroyo/ Celebrity Photo: 105; Kevin Winter/Celebrity Photo: 52

STYLISTS: Gayle Lederman, Jamie Caploe, author photo; Jessica Devin,
Roberta Caploe, author photo.

We dedicate this book with love to our parents,
Bob and Jeanne Caploe, who always told us,
"Why don't you turn off that damn TV and read
a book, for crying out loud!"

Contents

The ayes have it: *Melrose* denizens accept a People's Choice Award in 1993.

Acknowledgments

Many people helped us to bring *Melrose Confidential* to life. To all of them, we extend our most heartfelt thanks.

To Bill Wolfsthal, for getting us into this mess; Marcy Swingle, for helping us through the mess; Jodie Gould; Steve Robinson; Stuart Krichevsky; the always inspiring Robert Rorke; and the fabulous Enid Lewin.

Our rambunctious and enthusiastic family: David Caploe and Lyn Marini; Peter Caploe, Susan Grenrock and Max Caploe; Andrew, Susan and Tucker Caploe, Larry, Toni and Scott Scheflin; and Murray and Helen Scheflin.

Michael Maloney, for his constant feedback and riotous impressions.

A special thank you to Aaron Spelling, Darren Star, and the cast, crew, and staff of *Melrose Place*, who make the show the dazzling romp we love to watch.

ROBERTA CAPLOE THANKS:

Lynn Leahey and my colleagues at *Soap Opera Digest*.

Frank Tobin; Elyse Hibdon; Marcia Orcutt; Lauren Oliver; Paulette Cohn; Mary Andersen; Brenda Feldman; Mark Levine; Robert Waldron; Deirdre Martin; Jim Holmes; and Diane Brounstein.

My sister Jamie, for her willingness to try anything, including all varieties of takeout food.

Eric Weiss, for coming back into my life at precisely the right time, and filling it with joy.

JAMIE CAPLOE THANKS:

Julie Bannerman, for her sparkle and her faith in me; Ruth Sherman, for endless encouragement; Matt and Lisa Chanoff, for the great title suggestion; Kim Miller-Hershon, for cheering me on; Luba Reeves, for the sheer necessities of life; Faith Katkin, Carol Marque and Marushka Glissen, for our continuing friendships; Bernard Marque, for the snappy shots; Larry Scheflin, for launching me into cyberspace; Vic Ress, for his long answers to my short questions; Ron Bannerman, for the e-mail tips; and Fred Reeves, for responding to my desperate cyberspace queries with humor, speed and, always, a solution.

My sister, Roberta, for her generosity of spirit and for making this project a time of happiness and excitement.

My dear husband, Alan Scheflin; for believing in me long before I believed in myself; I treasure your love, kindness and brilliance.

My daughter, Hallie Caploe Scheflin, for her patience and understanding while her mother and aunt were busy scribbling.

"Sisters, sisters, there were never such devoted sisters."—Irving Berlin

July 8, 1992, seemed like any other day—the sun rose; birds tweeted; Bill Clinton got a haircut. But that evening, *Melrose Place* debuted, and broadcast history was made. It was a simple show, focusing on the travails of a group of twentysomething residents in a West Hollywood apartment house. No one that night, not even the powers that be who created the show, realized what they had unleashed.

Melrose Place was Fox Television's attempt to lasso the elusive Generation X. Aaron Spelling and Darren Star (the visionaries who were also behind *Beverly Hills 90210*) weren't the first TV heavyweights to realize that there was a gold mine in a show that would attract young adults. But instead of creating characters who were aimless mumblers, Spelling and Star decided to engage America's slackers, hackers, and nineties yuppies in a new way. They silhouetted eight struggling young adults against a most glamorous backdrop—the city of Los Angeles, home to movies, spectacular beaches, and sensational hunks and babes.

The original cast was a heavenly array of people with curves and bulges in all the right places. They included: construction worker Jake Hanson (Grant Show); advertising goddess in-training Alison Parker (Courtney Thorne-Smith); her platonic (oh, sure) starving writer roommate Billy Campbell (Andrew Shue); frisky aerobics teacher Rhonda Blair (Vanessa Williams); her roommate, wanna-be actress—and practicing waitress—Sandy Harling (Amy Locane); homosexual community activist and social worker Matt Fielding (Doug Savant); and building managers Michael Mancini (Thomas Calabro), a medical intern, and his wife Jane (Josie Bissett), an aspiring clothing designer.

The Star and Spelling prescription did the trick. *Melrose* characters chased their dreams and looked astoundingly gorgeous during the pursuit. Viewers identified with their confusion, setbacks, and fears, while

Star-crossed duo: Will Jo and Jake ever get it together?

simultaneously wishing they could compete with their luscious looks, sculpted bodies, and fashion-forward wardrobes.

A scant year later, *Melrose Place* had inspired imitations and parodies everywhere, from *Saturday Night Live* to *Seinfeld*. "King of all Media" Howard Stern tapes the show each week. People turn on the answering machine and have parties every Monday night so they can enjoy the *Melrose* antics with their friends. Do they need to get a life? Gosh, no. *Melrose Place* is simply too juicy a treat, too much of a giggly sin to give up. And here's how the sexy, lively, whirlwind began. . .

MELROSE
Confidential

Angst by the Pool

WANTED: ROOMMATE

Those lucky few who tuned into the very first *Melrose Place* episode may have thought they were watching *The Alison Parker Show*. Alison was a panicky whirlwind as she raced from apartment to apartment, trying to find out where her roommate Natalie had disappeared to in the middle of the night. As each complex resident answered the door, we were introduced to the gang.

Alison had to find a house-mate fast or she'd lose her digs. So, en route to her job as a receptionist at D&D Advertising, she hurriedly composed a want ad. A rambunctious puppy of a guy, Billy Campbell, answered her call—God knows, it wouldn't be the first time. Initially, Alison turned him down flat, but after the stream of pathetic losers that trailed to her door after him, she reconsidered. Billy moved in, and it was a game of one-on-one from the get-go. An obsessive Alison labeled every item in the fridge, while Billy wondered if she'd lay low when he brought dates home.

After a rush parking job that left a ding in her boss Hal's car, Alison found that her bad luck led to an invitation from Hal himself to a product-launch party. Visions of ultra-hip Calvin Klein ads filled her head as she navigated among the hoi polloi at the rooftop soirée. Unfortunately, visions of Alison naked were fueling a tipsy Hal, who later wormed his way into her apartment. When Billy overheard the old man's sweet talk, he bounded into the living room in his boxers—and nothing else—to defend his "wife" Alison. Expecting gratitude, Billy instead got a great view of Alison's well-chiseled chin in the air as she stomped away. From that moment on, we were treated to many scenes of a shirtless Billy sparring with a defensive, stubborn Alison.

At D&D, Alison hungered to sink her teeth into a real advertising campaign. She met up with Rick, mailroom flunky and son of one of the firm's leading clients, a sunscreen manufacturer. Alison enthusiastically

On a plane to Toronto, a passenger once passed Thomas Calabro a napkin that read: "How could you do that to Jane?!" You ain't seen nothing yet, honey.

confided in him about the humdinger of a campaign she'd dreamed up for the product. But her high hopes fell flat when Rick scampered over to the big brass and passed off her proposal as his own. Innocent Ali reeled in shock. Lucy Cabot, her older and wiser boss, sat the wide-eyed phone-girl down for a heart-to-heart about the wicked ways of the real world. By the time Alison's feathers were smoothed, she was ready to take the second chance Lucy offered to pitch ideas to the sunscreen client.

Back on the home front, Alison dithered over "Betsy," her old wreck of a car. Dewy-eyed at the prospect of buying a zippy red convertible, she made a number of lame attempts to pawn off the clunker on unsuspecting buyers. Billy hovered, dishing up a mess of macho, auto-savvy posturing. (Geez, why didn't she ask Jake Hanson for help? That guy's a *mechanic*, for God's sake.) In the end, the idea of hoodwinking someone in order to unload the junk heap was too much for Alison, to say nothing of the car's sentimental value—heck, she'd lost her virginity in the damn thing. Let the engine seize and the paint rust—Betsy stayed in the garage.

Though no one could satisfy her exacting housekeeping standards, Alison was determined to make Billy pull his weight in the clean-up department. Ever agreeable, Billy chose to make his mark in the laundry room. The soapy load was burping along just fine, until he came across Alison's bra. Even though Billy resisted the urge to do his best RuPaul imitation, Alison was not amused.

Parker soon perked up when she met Keith Gray, a self-proclaimed bigwig with an environmental organization. Naturally, Keith was put under the patented *Melrose* microscope at Shooters, the local hangout. (By this point, Billy held his nose any time he was introduced to a new beau of Alison's. Oh, you didn't know that? Go to the back of the class.)

Our usually hyper-motivated huckster was besotted with her new love. When she started blowing off work to be with Keith, everyone from her boss Lucy to her pals wondered, "Just how good *is* he in bed?" Even the news that Keith was married didn't stop Alison. She staked out his house when his wife Lily came to town, then sped away when the "other woman" spotted her.

After much hand-wringing, Alison knew she had to walk away from the whole sordid mess. Though she pined for Keith, she kept away from him.

Heartache soon turned into real physical pain when Alison learned she needed gynecological surgery. Since her insurance wouldn't cover the bills, intern Michael Mancini pitched in and arranged for her to be admitted to the hospital as a teaching patient. Billy stood by loyally, spending a quiet Christmas with his favorite friend.

Meanwhile, Jake Hanson had his hands full unloading Kelly Taylor, the underage glamour puss who kept popping up from nearby *Beverly Hills 90210*. The lovesick lass had a Texas-size crush, but between Jake's reluctance to commit statutory rape and her coterie of friends loitering one diner booth away, the romance fizzled. (After all, she was just a spin-off sweetie; time for her to cruise back to her cushy *90210* digs.)

Like everyone else at *Melrose*, Jake's love life hurtled along at warp speed. After Kelly split, Jake discovered he still had an open invitation for sleep-overs at neighbor Sandy Harling's. They two-stepped back and forth over reigniting their old flame.

Love doesn't pay the rent, however. So when an old squeeze, Perry, offered to include Jake in a high-priced art scam she was running, Jake listened. It sounded enticing, but Perry's cocaine-fueled shenanigans scared him off. When keeping double latte orders straight at a chi-chi coffee bar proved not to be his cup of tea, either, Jake decided to sell off his most prized possession—his motorcycle. At the bike shop, his luck turned around when the owner was more interested in Jake's mechanic skills than his used wheels. Yahoo! A regularly scheduled paycheck!

Poolside tongues immediately began to wag when Jake and Alison spent the night at his apartment. If anyone had bothered to peek in the window, they would have seen how innocent the goings-on were, however. A bashful Jake had sought Alison's assistance in cramming for his G.E.D. exam. Embarrassed that he'd never finished high school, he wanted to keep the upcoming test under wraps.

Of course, learnin' often leads to yearnin'—at least on *Melrose*. On a late-night motorcycle-spin-study-break, Alison and Jake did smooch it up, high atop Mulholland Drive. Before long, naturally, the cat was out of the bag.

After Jake returned from his ordeal by multiple choice, Alison dragged him to Shooters, where the usual suspects were waiting to congratulate the studly scholar. Sandy had organized the impromptu graduation fete, though she took time out to berate Jake for causing Billy major love-anxiety as he imagined Alison in Jake's arms.

Sandy did help out Jake later when his mother Stella made a guest appearance at his surprise birthday party. Mom moved in for what she hoped would be an extended visit, but a hardhearted Jake was in no mood to forgive Stella's many drunken sins. At Sandy's urging, he did finally make peace before Stella hopped a bus out of town.

Yet another shocker for Jake was the news that his old girlfriend, Colleen, had a son named David—whose daddy was none other than our favorite grease monkey. After much soul searching, advice from fellow *'Placers* and seeing the boy's happy life with Colleen and her new husband, Jake relinquished his parental rights so David could be adopted by his mother's new man.

HI-IMPACT

Rhonda Blair huffed and puffed herself into a tizzy over her date with Daniel, a student in her aerobics class. Between Jane Mancini's fashion tips and Matt Fielding's cheerleading, Rhonda floated off for the night on cloud nine; before midnight she drooped home, disheartened that Daniel had wanted her to help him sell a line of vitamins, not fall in love.

There were bigger demons for her to face down when a dance troupe came to town. She had been invited to audition for the company previously, but had faked an injury to avoid the anxiety of possibly failing to make the cut. This time, Rhonda was determined to overcome her fears. Her dancing dazzled 'em—but Rhonda surprised everyone by turning down the offer. Proving to herself she could make the grade was reward enough.

Rhonda did not make the grade with her new roommate, Carrie. At first Rhonda was bemused by Carrie's nonstop alphabetizing, stacking, and spraying. But it got to be a little too much when Carrie practically had a fit after Rhonda neglected to scour a frying pan to Carrie's spic 'n' span specifications. Ms. Clean Crazy packed up her vacuum and zoomed off.

When romance did come around again, Rhonda took the long way home. Terrence Haggardy had it all—looks, charm, oodles of cash, and undying devotion to his lady. He had even picked out a dream house for them. But instead of running into Terrence's arms, she ran from them. Rhonda, that hopeless romantic, had come down with a severe case of commitment phobia.

The reappearance of neat freak Carrie as Terrence's decorator prompted Rhonda to reconsider her case of cold feet. As the two women sparred over every fabric swatch and paint chip, Rhonda couldn't help but recognize Terrence for the prize he was. In a very nineties twist, she proposed to her fella, and he happily accepted.

WRITE OR WRONG

Aspiring writer Billy, having already abandoned the plan of supporting himself as an Arthur Murray dance instructor, found that cab driving fed

Raging Bull

His namesake must be Jake LaMotta. Mr. Hanson sure ends up in more than his share of brawls, with hardly any provocation required. We offer this short list of scuffles:

★ While waiting at the unemployment office, Jake took umbrage at the clerk's treatment of a Latina on line and ended up getting arrested for assault.

★ Sandy's unwanted suitor Paul got slapped around by Jake as a message to stop hounding her.

★ After Matt got jumped by a gang of gay bashers, Jake suggested they grab some baseball bats and knock some sense into the bastards. Matt called the cops instead.

★ Kyle, a rude customer at the bike shop, got knocked around by an irate Jakester.

★ In a fit of frustration following the fire at Jake's Bikes, he trashed a refrigerator and scared the crap out of Jo.

★ Best man Jake bopped Billy smack on the jaw after finding out the groom-to-be had slept with Amanda.

★ Iowa hick Hank got one of Jake's patented punches, which he really deserved, since he'd shoved a pregnant Jo down the stairs.

★ After rescuing a hapless Sydney from a "black bra" contest at a bar, our hero had to fight off a drunken creep who followed them out to the parking lot.

his hormones as well as his bank account. The first of his many fare-thee-well encounters was with Marcy, an eager babe who lost no time insinuating herself with the pack around the pool. She departed the premises in tears when Billy confessed that he planned to stay in love's slow lane.

Another passionate patron was Dawn, a stand-up comic and single mom. She and Billy had their little fling, but he was clearly too much of a kid himself to contemplate stepping in as a stepdad. He dropped her off and returned to the on-ramp.

Cab driving lost its fascination for Billy when he got stranded and then a gang of kids roughed him up in South Central Los Angeles. Even Rhonda's impassioned defense of "those people," whom Billy stereotyped and ridiculed, couldn't convince him to stay behind the wheel. Faster than you can say "rewrite," he'd landed a gig penning a column for *Melrose Weekly*, the neighborhood free press.

At a poolside party to celebrate his new position, it began to dawn on Billy that his life wasn't really fodder for an exciting column, unless he wanted to write a piece on the peaks and pitfalls of never wearing a shirt. Anxious to wow 'em with tall tales, he corralled Jake and Matt to throw caution—and their bodies—to the wind with him and go bungee jumping.

But frightening flashbacks of being terrified atop the high-dive as a child froze Billy in his tracks. The images even haunted him in nightmares, giving roomie Alison a chance to comfort her friend, and giving him time to call off the whole escapade. Rippling muscles notwithstanding, Billy showed his sensitive side when he turned in his first column, which proclaimed, "It's okay for men to be scared."

"Scared" didn't begin to describe Billy's state of mind when he had to face his folks in Palm Springs. If his professional life hadn't taken off within a year, Billy'd promised them that he'd chuck his writing career and join his pop, Big Bill, in his furniture emporium. As phrases like "Would you like to see this chaise in a chintz?" crowded his head, Billy cooked up a dilly of a diversion. He dragged Alison to his father's birthday bash, and cast her in the starring role of his girlfriend. (Actually, that would be moving backwards, since he'd already pretended they were husband and wife.)

> "The appeal of *Melrose Place* is the unexpected. The good girl can become the bad girl in one episode. I think people tune in to see who is going to do what to whom next. It's campy, but fun. The characters could be your best friends in real life, but the things they say and do are a total fantasy."—Dick Clark

Over the hors d'oeuvres, a stunned Alison watched her status soar from mere significant other to big-time literary agent with the power to send her beau's career skyrocketing. Pretty amazing, especially since she'd given Billy a brutally blunt assessment of his first screenplay; namely, that it stunk. After much bedlam, Billy was forced to endure an endless day among the sofas and settees. By the time he'd cursed out a customer, dear old dad was convinced Junior was not cut out for life amid armoires and end tables. Billy happily reaffirmed his commitment to his Art.

Back in L.A., he continued to starve as an artist. Figuring plastic money could buy him time (and printer paper for his computer), he applied for a credit card and was rejected. Then he remembered all those pesky student loans he'd taken out and never repaid—for dorm room essentials like a neat stereo system. Mom and Pop were sympathetic, but kept their checkbooks clamped shut. Billy showed them, and got a full-time job, writing for *Escapade* magazine.

When a monster toothache took over Billy's life, Alison came to the rescue with a brilliant plan—go to the dentist, she told him. Back at home with a mouthful of cotton and a body pumped with drugs, Billy soon slipped deep into an erotic dream starring his luscious roomie. Alison caught the drift of his fantasy when she heard him moaning her name as he fondled a pillow.

THE NEWLYWED GAME

The big exception to the *Melrose* date-o-rama at the show's start was the young married Mancinis. Their most pressing romantic problem? Finding the time and energy for sex. Michael put in long hours at the hospital, and Jane worked a nine-to-five or later stint at a local boutique. Add on their duties as sink-uncloggers and lightbulb-changers at the apartment house, and you can see how the two rarely had room in their schedule for nookie. And here's a surprise—Jane's engine revved even hotter than Michael's.

When the pooped-out medico disappointed his wife by not remembering *exactly* when he fell in love with her, Jane slipped off her wedding band and slipped into Shooters to try her luck. The singles scene proved dismal, and she scurried back home.

There, Jane had a bigger problem than being married and trying to date at the same time—she was pregnant. Fearing Michael's negative reaction and unsure of her own, Jane trooped off to the nearest family planning clinic amid a gaggle of girlfriends. The secret soon spread like poison ivy, and Rhonda let the info slip to Michael. Just as Jane feared, Michael was a not-so-proud-papa-to-be. Eventually the couple calmed down, and made plans to welcome their new addition. But Michael's fumbling at childbirth class, complete with breaking the arm off a practice baby doll, made Jane question his prospective parenting abilities.

Mother Nature took matters into her own hands when Jane miscarried, while a sulking Michael was stuck at the hospital. Mancini's hormones were on a slow drip, thanks to the new attentions of Dr. Kimberly Shaw. The spark between the two M.D.'s signaled the demise of the Mancini marriage.

Complications continued as Jane's younger sister Sydney blew in from Chicago. The visit turned into a family feud, with Syd dogging her sister's every move at home and at work. She tried to vamp Michael and unseat Jane at her new job as a junior designer for fashion tyrant Kay Beacon. Exasperated, Jane ordered Syd out of the apartment and the state.

Michael's rendezvous with Kimberly began to eat up what little free time he had. When yet another "work emergency" dragged him away from his wife, a bewildered Jane found herself on a date with Michael's old college friend, Sam Towler. Why am I kissing another man? she wondered.

News of Jane's extramarital buss led Michael to see Kimberly as more than a naked body underneath a white coat. Before you could say "young doctors in love," they were. No hospital closet was safe from their amorous exploits. Jane reached the end of her wifely rope, and by season's end the only place she and Michael were going together was Divorce Court.

H O L L Y W O O D   H O R R O R   S H O W

Sandy kept busy trying to build an acting career, which was harder than she'd planned. When she finally landed a gig in a low-budget slasher flick, the director wanted her to bare some skin while she screamed. Sandy did it, but she wasn't too happy—and boy, was she grouchy to all her friends.

Things went from bad to worse when Sandy acquired an overeager suitor. Paul picked up Ms. Harling in a trendy Melrose shop and—whammo—they made a date. The evening was a flop, and she unloaded the guy. Or so she thought. Soon Paul was parading his pecs by the pool and her friends were busily insisting she give him another chance.

The word "no" simply didn't exist for the nurseryman/loverboy. First, he fanned out a flotilla of lilies in the pool. Next, he bombarded Sandy's answering machine with countless messages. The final straw came when he strewed her bed with a blanket of roses. The petal profusion did not sway Sandy's southern heart; instead she sought refuge—again—in Jake's loving arms. When Jake finally let her go, he duked it out with Paul. In the end, Sandy proved she could clean up her own messes (though there was the amusing sight of Michael and Jane fishing those pesky lilies out of the pool), when she told Paul off for good at the nursery.

Sandy's dreams of hitting it big finally began to pay off. She landed a juicy role on a New York soap, *Forever and Tomorrow*, playing Aviva Lester, a beautiful neurosurgeon. Sandy packed her bags and waved good-bye to the California sunshine.

PLAYING THE FIELDING

Rhonda's best buddy Matt kept himself busy at the halfway house for teens where he was a social worker. He loved the kids and his job. Not everything was sunshine and lollipops for Matt, though. Late one night, he was attacked by a gang of homophobic goons outside a dance club. He somehow managed to drag himself back to the apartment complex, where Jake took over and got his pal to the emergency room. The less than helpful attitude of the cops led Jake to bellow his outrage at meaningless violence (a bit of a surprise, coming from the winner of the "most likely to have a fistfight" competition).

A visit from a police investigator pinning down some details about the melee tipped off Matt's boss, who gave Matt the boot. Jake urged him to take action (think baseball bats), but Fielding consulted with a lawyer about suing for sexual discrimination instead.

Soon he discovered that justice carried a high price—$5,000 to be exact. That was the fee attorney Sarah Goldstein required, up front. Jake, that fount of suggestions, convinced Matt to call his parents for the cash. Like Billy and his credit card debacle, Matt got sympathy, a pat on the head, and no bucks. He decided to make the ultimate Los Angelino sacrifice and sell his car. But lawyer Sarah told him it wasn't necessary. As long as she could gain notoriety from the publicity the case would generate, she'd waive her usual fees.

Matt was eventually offered a settlement of $10,000 and his old job back. Ms. Goldstein wanted to hold out for a bigger payoff and more press, but Matt put an end to the proceedings. To prove his heart was in the right place, he donated his cash to a legal defense fund to fight discrimination.

DANCING IN THE DARK ROOM

The final person to move into the complex during the first season was Jo Reynolds, a smoky-voiced, dark-haired photographer. She hinted at an unhappy life—and husband—left behind in New York when she met Alison in the laundry room one night. The two bonded over a bottle of tequila and scampered over to Shooters for a rowdy pool match with some of the guys. Jo's cool action with a cue stick impressed the crowd.

The only one in the *Place* not immediately smitten with the black-clad New Yorker was Jake. Their first introduction took place when he lumbered to her door wrapped in a patch of terry cloth to grouse that she'd ruined his shower.

Towel-dry, Jake reassessed his new neighbor and admitted she was a lovely slice of pie. He readily agreed to help her sell a bracelet to raise funds. But its inscription—"Beth"—got him into trouble when a potential buyer assumed Jake was trafficking in stolen goods.

Jo caused Jake to scratch his head again when she roared off on his motorcycle, turning up the next morning with a police escort. Seemed Jake was going to get a ticket for "letting" her use the bike without a license. Attempting to make it up to him, Jo treated Jake to dinner out, where he again got confused when someone who knew her called her "Beth."

Finally, Jo 'fessed up. Charles, her alcoholic, society-whirl husband, used to beat her up when he was looped, and she had to get away. Before he could murmur "poor baby," Jake was soothing Jo's troubles away with kisses and hugs galore.

Hubby Charles tracked her down and begged her for another chance. Jake waited patiently while Jo made up her mind. She not only returned to Jake; but also used her divorce settlement to set him up in his own shop, "Jake's Bikes."

Bad-girl Perry popped up again and tossed some icy water on the new couple with the tip that she had AIDS. Jake and Jo sweated out the wait for their test results together. They were hugely relieved when the exams came back negative.

Soon after that crisis, Karen, a model friend of Jo's, landed in L.A. She propositioned both Jo and Jake. They politely declined her offer of a ménage à trois—living at *Melrose Place* was enough of a group grope for them.

WAYWARD WOODWARD

And now, the moment you've all been waiting for. Ladies and gentlemen, please welcome Amanda Woodward. Somehow that show had muddled along without her for months. But as soon as advertising whiz and "older" woman (we mean early thirties, folks) Amanda sashayed onto the scene, excitement pinged and fizzed all over the place.

As a high-powered ad executrix, Amanda made Alison's ascent from receptionist to assistant account executive eventful. No sooner was Parker promoted than she was ordered to round up a photographer in two days for an important shoot. Every known professional in L.A. was booked, so Alison hired Jo to photograph the men's underwear ad.

In no time, Alison and Jo's artistic visions clashed. Jo wanted to go the avant garde route, and have the tennis star who was posing for them, Rex Weldon, *hold* the BVDs to coyly cover his manly gifts. The client was appalled, and insisted that the nude pix be nixed. Alison endured a nasty tongue-lashing from Amanda; Jo rolled her eyes in creative disgust.

Amanda knew how to play as well as work. She took one look at Billy and smacked her lips in anticipation. She invited him and Alison to her family's rustic mountain getaway, where they played a mean game of Truth or Dare. Amanda snagged Billy, while Alison steamed.

Alison's romance with Keith lurched back to the "on" mode, even when he was transferred to Seattle. It looked like he was finally going to start a new life without his wife, so Alison took the plunge and moved with him. She rushed back to L.A. to console Billy, however, as soon as she heard that his father had died. Realizing how much she missed Billy and her life in the City of Angels, Alison chucked Keith and crawled back to D&D as a lowly receptionist. (You didn't think Amanda would give her her old job back, did you?)

At a business retreat in Palm Springs, Amanda did her level best to keep Billy as her own treat. But our Billy-boy drove to the desert, evaded Ms. Woodward, and finally, finally, finally, declared his love to Alison. The two made passionate love at long last. The *Melrose Place* audience cheered—and the folks in the adjoining hotel room didn't get much sleep.

Not one to be outdone, Amanda splashed cold water on the lovebirds with the sobering bulletin that she was pregnant with Billy's baby and intended to keep the child. But after she miscarried, the path was cleared for Alison and Billy to wallow in their newfound romance.

Soon, a bigger hurdle than size-three Amanda cast a shadow over their lives. Keith had returned. But he'd changed, just a little. Now he was an obsessive, stalking psycho who'd stop at nothing to keep Alison for himself. Seeing Billy's attachment to his beloved, Keith did what any twisted monster would do—he attacked Billy from behind with a whack of a tire iron. Trouble was brewing like a bitter cup of coffee. *Melrose Place* had finally found its way.

Courtney Thorne-Smith

FROM PROM QUEEN TO DRAMA QUEEN

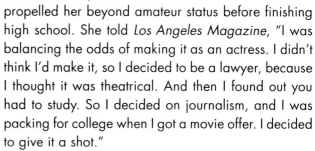

Courtney Thorne-Smith's no fool. As a teen star who grew up to be—gasp—normal and still employable, she thanks her lucky stars for *Melrose Place* and the role of Alison Parker. As she told *Rolling Stone*, "You know, it's a job, so be grateful, go buy a house, and every time you sit in it, think, 'My job got me this house.' Then go right back to work."

Professional acting opportunities came quickly for Thorne-Smith, who hails from California's tony Marin County. Plucked from the Ensemble Theater Company, the rigorous academic training program of Tamalpais High School in Mill Valley, Thorne-Smith's drive and enthusiasm propelled her beyond amateur status before finishing high school. She told *Los Angeles Magazine*, "I was balancing the odds of making it as an actress. I didn't think I'd make it, so I decided to be a lawyer, because I thought it was theatrical. And then I found out you had to study. So I decided on journalism, and I was packing for college when I got a movie offer. I decided to give it a shot."

Her decision was a smart one. Thorne-Smith's first professional work unspooled in the feature film *Lucas*, a well-received 1985 coming-of-age charmer about a misfit finding his way in the cruel world of teenagers. The actress won the role after responding to an open casting call—and it quickly set her off on the right foot. In a cast that included fellow newcomer Winona Ryder (who began the production under her real name, Winona Horowitz), Thorne-Smith turned the right heads as the cheerleader girlfriend to Charlie Sheen's obnoxious football-hero stud.

Her career began to snowball. Television movies followed, such as ABC's *Infidelity*, USA's *Breach of Conduct*, and Disney's *The Thanksgiving Promise*, which featured three generations of the Bridges clan, from Lloyd to son Beau to grandson Jordan. On the big screen, Thorne-Smith cornered the college-cutie market in *Summer School*, *Revenge of the Nerds II: Nerds in Paradise*, and *Welcome to 18*.

Melrose Place was not Thorne-Smith's first series. She was picked to appear as Stacy Hamilton on the short-lived 1986 sitcom *Fast Times* (based on the feature *Fast Times at Ridgemont High*). She was a regular on *Family Ties*'s creator Gary David Goldberg's 1988 series *Day by Day*, as Kristin Carlson, the brainy beauty who turned the head of a teenage boy, Ross (played by Christopher Barnes). Soon her seductive powers were put to a greater test when she appeared in six memorable episodes of *L.A. Law* as the Laker Girl who busted up Michael Kuzak (Harry Hamlin) and Grace Van Owen (Susan Dey).

These short-lived roles were a far cry from the unrelenting spotlight that was cast by *Melrose Place*, however. While Thorne-Smith jumped at the job, the unexpected media scrutiny and audience fervor took its toll on her by the end of the first season. "I was sick all the time. I didn't know how I was going to make it," she told *Rolling Stone*.

But Thorne-Smith weathered the *Melrose* monsoon. Even when that *other* blonde, Heather Locklear, came aboard and garnered the lion's share of the spotlight, Thorne-Smith has been both gracious and generous about life in the *'Place*. Though the gossip rags would like to invent a rivalry between Thorne-Smith and Locklear, none exists. In reality, Thorne-Smith marvels at her costar. "We'll be out to lunch and Heather will say, 'Yes, I'd like fried zucchini circles with ranch dressing.' And I'll be having a tuna salad with fat-free dressing. I hate her. . . . People like to think she's like Amanda. I didn't think that, but there's no way I expected her to be so funny and kind and quick and self-deprecating. No way. You think, with the way she looks, why should she develop a personality?" Thorne-Smith wondered aloud to *Rolling Stone*.

Away from the set, Thorne-Smith putts her worries away on the golf course. "It brings up every possible emotional problem you've ever had," she joked to *Entertainment Weekly*, "Everyone is standing there waiting for you, and if you mess up, the pressure is overwhelming."

In a refreshing switch from good-girl Alison, Thorne-Smith got to chew up the scenery in the 1995 NBC movie *Beauty's Revenge*, as a psycho beauty queen whose crown fit a tad too tight. It must have been satisfying to play the woman who dishes out the crap, for a change.

Thorne-Smith is also sharp enough not to confuse her real life with the parts she plays. And that's a good thing. As she told *TV Guide*, "If this [*Melrose Place*] were real life, I don't think you could survive it."

Quick Comebacks and Disasters

Michael is in jail for stalking Amanda; Sydney comes to visit.

SYDNEY: Michael, you look terrible. Have you lost weight?

MICHAEL: No, Syd. The guys and I order out for burgers and beer every night. What do you think?

A little later:

SYDNEY: Here's a tip: keep your back to the wall.

Sydney to Kimberly, who's fresh out of the psychiatric hospital.

SYDNEY: How's the electroshock going? It's putting an attractive curl in your hair.

At Peter's medical board hearing.

AMANDA: I was stabbed with a hypodermic, almost cut open, badly treated for my cancer, and sexually harassed. As far as I'm concerned, all the doctors who treated me should have their licenses taken away. And if you don't revoke Dr. Burns's license, I will not only sue Wilshire Memorial, but I'll sue each and every board member in this room for reckless endangerment. Now if that's all, I have a wedding to attend.

When Jake goes to Las Vegas to rescue Sydney from Chris Marchette, Jane's double-crossing Australian boyfriend, he finds her dressed to the nines, eating a sumptuous room service meal:

JAKE: For a kidnapping victim, you look pretty good.

When Kimberly's about to blow up the complex:

KIMBERLY: It's not what it looks like—it's much worse.

Peter has just found out that Kimberly stole Jo's baby.

MICHAEL: You wanted to see me?

PETER: I wanted to kill you, but fortunately, that moment has passed.

Then Michael has pangs of conscience and returns Jo's baby to her.

MICHAEL: Merry Christmas, Jo. You got what you wanted. Stay the hell out of our lives.

Matt visits Sydney in jail for attempted murder of Michael.

SYDNEY: It's them, the two doctors from hell; they're trying to get me executed.

MATT: Syd, you can't be executed for attempted murder.

SYDNEY: Great. That's supposed to make me feel better. I'll just rot the rest of my life away in prison with the Manson girls.

In the very first episode, Alison tells Billy she doesn't think they should be roommates.

BILLY: Fine, fine. Probably wouldn't have worked out anyway. You're uptight, you're high strung, overjudgmental. My god, it would be like living with my mother.

And much to Alison's chagrin, Billy comes up short with the first month's rent when he does move in.

ALISON: Billy, this may come as a shock to you, but I am not living with you on the basis of your stunning good looks and sparkling personality. I'm living with you because you promised to come up with your half of the rent promptly and in full.

Drug-smuggler Reed is dragging Jo away to Mexico on the boat.

REED: You already got your mind made up about me, don't you?

JO: You locked me in a dark hole for two days. What do you expect?

REED: I explained that. That was for your own good.

Kimberly's back from the dead and Sydney's married to Michael.

KIMBERLY: Now you get this clear, you opportunistic little bitch, if anything's old news around here it's you and if you think that shotgun marriage you arranged is gonna protect you, then you are dumber than you look.

———

Alison invites Billy to lunch to accept his marriage proposal.

BILLY: Did you ever notice that every time you spring for lunch we end up eating hot dogs in the park?

ALISON: What can I say? I like the simple things in life.

BILLY: No, you're just cheap.

———

Billy wants to ask Jake to be his best man, not knowing Jake has just found out Billy slept with Amanda.

BILLY: Jake Hanson, you've been a great friend of mine the last couple of years and I want you to be my best man.

JAKE: Go to hell, you son of a bitch.

———

After the apartment complex is bombed, Peter invites Amanda to stay at his place.

PETER: I'd like for you to stay at my place tonight. I'll cook you a nice breakfast in the morning. . .

AMANDA: Like hell. I'd rather sleep on a grate.

———

A moment later:

SYDNEY: Amanda just turned down free bed and breakfast.

AMANDA: Nothing's free, Syd; you'll never understand that.

———

Kimberly and Peter have a chat about Michael.

KIMBERLY: Scratch the surface of something that's twisted and you're bound to find Michael's ugly little smile.

———

Jake finds Amanda sweeping up after the bombing.

AMANDA: I just hope my insurance covers mad bombers.

———

Michael gives Peter his opinion of Kimberly after the bombing.

MICHAEL: We're talking about a psycho who nearly burned down a city block. If anybody deserves to be shackled to a steam pipe in hell, it's her.

———

How Come?

★ With all that sex going on, no one ever has beard burn?

★ Billy sat straight-faced at a D&D meeting with Alison, Amanda, and Brooke, and no one ever mentioned the fact that he'd slept with every woman at the table?

★ Billy was shirtless for the entire first season?

★ The rent is a puny $800 per month?

★ Jane doesn't design some decent outfits for Sydney?

★ Not a single friend or neighbor attended the funeral of Matt's father, not even good buddy Michael?

★ Alison got drunk at a business lunch, launched a food fight at a D&D party, and took more personal time than a chairman of the board, but wasn't fired?

Paul Scalisi, Owner of *Pane Caldo Restaurant* in Los Angeles:

Q. Is it realistic that Jake didn't keep his own books or use a computer, and that he got intimately involved with his bookkeeper?

A. In the restaurant business, a lot of people don't keep books, and trust their accountants. And accountants do rip people off by getting their clients to give them the "power of signature." That's why I do all my own books, even though I have an accountant, also.

In this business, it's also easy to get involved with people you work with. I once dated one of my cashiers. You know, the moment hits, the desk is there . . . who knows?

★ Billy, Alison, and Amanda don't carpool to work even though they all live in the same place?

★ Amanda wears skirts shorter than a sound bite and nobody looks twice?

and later on:

MICHAEL: You're a surgeon. What're you going to do for her—cut out the bad part of her brain? There won't be anything left.

Then Sydney throws in her opinion:

SYDNEY: If you could give me one good reason why you're so hell bent on saving her. I mean, God, Peter, Kimberly is a vicious monster with so many screws loose she could start a hardware store.

Then again, Amanda applies the same observation to Sydney.

AMANDA: Honestly, Sydney's mouth is as loose as her screws.

Sydney won't dance with Jake when he's drunk at Shooters after Jess died.

SYDNEY: Unlike you, Jake, when tragedy strikes I don't click up my heels and wrap my lips around a bottle.

Matt's up on murder charges; Amanda consoles him.

AMANDA: Oh, Matt, I haven't had the chance to say this to you, but I heard about your problems and I'm really sorry . . . and I want you to know that while some people may not feel comfortable with your presence here, you have my full support. I mean, the way I see it, even if you did murder that woman, it was clearly a crime of passion. I mean, it's not as though you're a serial killer.

Brooke blackmails Amanda about her long lost husband Jack.

BROOKE: I expected skeletons, but nothing on this grand a scale. Faking your own death to get out of a marriage. Changing your name. Changing your whole identity. Only you could pull off something this wild.

Sydney delivers some files to Peter at home. Kimberly answers the door.

KIMBERLY: Sydney, don't be afraid. I'm much better now. Why don't you come in and have a drink and I'll tell you all about it?

SYDNEY: You may have fooled those medical dimwits, but I know that you are still a murdering, mutant freak.

Then Peter consoles Kimberly when he hears what happened.

PETER: Sydney isn't exactly the poster child for sanity.

And Sydney rushes her report back to Michael.

SYDNEY: It was so creepy, Michael. Kimberly tried to get me inside the house. And she has this weird gizmo thing on her wrist.

MICHAEL: A monitor?

SYDNEY: I don't know, I think she uses it to beam up to the mother ship.

Then Sydney gets a scare when she reads Kimberly's file.

SYDNEY: Have you seen this? Kimberly is completely cracked. She makes Sybil look like Marie Osmond.

Jack Parezi, Amanda's husband, lets Billy know he should back off.

JACK: You know, yesterday, you were merely irritating; today you're a pain in the ass.

Amanda throws a party when the apartments are fixed up after the bombing. Who should invite herself but Kimberly?

AMANDA: Have all the demons in hell come to torment me?

Kimberly is terrified after "Henry" materializes in the laundry room at Amanda's party. Michael and Sydney are thrilled their plan is working.

SYDNEY: Coming apart at your coming out party?

MICHAEL: Mmm—looks to me like a bad case of the heebie-jeebies.

Michael accuses Peter of falsifying Jack's hospital report for all the wrong reasons.

MICHAEL: Hey, someone put a world of hurt into that guy and my guess is that it was you. Now what did he do, doc? Take your money at the golf course? Insult your manhood? Or maybe you just couldn't stand the idea of him getting back into Amanda's pants.

Kimberly calls in to Dr. Joyce Brothers radio show talking about Michael.

KIMBERLY: Dr. Brothers, this man is one notch below the Antichrist.

Grant Show

Grant Show grew up far from the glitter of Hollywood. Born in Detroit, but raised in rural areas around Santa Cruz, California, Show learned early to be a resourceful loner. His parents indulged in a quasi-hippie, back-to-nature phase that included staking homesteads some twenty miles from school and potential playmates. Just getting back and forth could take up most of a day. For a two-year stretch, the family got along without electricity. Show and his sister Kelly rode motorcycles and horses while roaming the mountains. Clearly, the experience molded him into a person who can enjoy his own company (he loves to run, lift weights, and play golf), and that sense of solitude feeds his character's more edgy loneliness.

Another parallel between actor and role is their blue-collar backgrounds. Grant's dad passed on his mechanic's training to his son, so all of Jake's grease monkey puttering on the set is authentic—hand him a wrench and he's a happy boy. Show is well aware that this gritty aspect of Jake's background is always at the root of his character's relationships. When asked what attraction binds Jake and Amanda, he told *Rolling Stone*: "Even though Amanda's got more money than most of the chicks he's gone with, she's still just white trash, like he is."

Show's first big acting break came in 1984 when he was hired to play Officer Rick Hyde—a Jake-like down to earth character—on the soap opera *Ryan's Hope*. In 1987, when his contract with the show was up, he poured all of his savings from *Ryan's Hope* into a grueling, but gratifying, year at the London Academy of Music and Dramatic Art. The training he received there boosted his acting technique, as well as his self-confidence. Exclusive and intense (outside employment was prohibited), the program gave Show the chance to immerse himself in the serious study of Shakespeare and Shaw (and we don't mean Kimberly).

Show put his newly-honed theater skills to the test in a well-received run as Terry Malloy in *On the Waterfront* at the Cleveland Playhouse in the fall of 1988, as well as *The Boys of Winter* on Broadway. Even rave reviews won't buy subway tokens, however, and Show eventually found himself making the audition rounds once more. In 1989, he appeared in the short-lived NBC drama *True Blue*, a cop show filmed in New York City. Other television and big screen movies came along, but productions fizzled before they flashed. On a humorous note, CBS utilized Show's services for a TV pilot that went nowhere—at first. After *Melrose* began to take off, however, the network aired the movie, calling it *Coopersmith*.

By the time Spelling Productions was casting Jake Hanson, Show knew the audition process inside out. He knew how great the odds were against being cast. And he knew he was tired of having to paint houses to make enough money for the mortgage. So with nothing to lose, he bluntly asked the producers at his second audition what he could do that would separate him from the gang of 300 T-shirted wonders who were parading by.

Whatever he did, it worked. Aaron Spelling and Company chose Jake as the character who'd travel to the land of *Beverly Hills 90210* to romance Kelly Taylor (Jennie Garth) and hopefully introduce a slew of new fans to the pleasures of *Melrose Place*. The media frenzy surrounding the show's start-up planted Show on the covers of *TV Guide* and *People* before *Melrose* even debuted. Show took the heat with grace and wit. As he told *Rolling Stone*: ". . . the minute I walked on the set and saw that they'd built a real pool, I had the feeling we'd be around for a while. Forget about actors, man; *pools* aren't cheap."

Show has watched *Melrose* find its footing with a somewhat jaundiced eye. "We were a bunch of saps the first season. The episode would be like, 'Jake goes back and gets his diploma.' I mean, who *gives* a shit? There was no tension. No conflict . . . I just remember begging for something to play. *Anything*," he said to *Rolling Stone*.

While Show doesn't want to look the *Melrose* gift horse in the mouth, he does distance himself from the media circus that surrounds the now-megahit phenomenon (although he *has* publicly confessed to wearing silk boxer shorts). He was the only cast member who declined to pose for a cover photo shoot for the fall 1995 *Entertainment Weekly* special issue devoted to the show. As the editors wrote in their profile, "Don't bring up his stud image, his on-screen conquests, his off-screen steady. In fact, don't bring up anything."

Well, okay, we won't.

Michael's tuned in and calls in his own opinion.

MICHAEL: Now, listen, you zipper-headed mutant. You tried to kill me twice. Then you blew up an entire building because your imaginary playmate told you naughty people lived in there.

Sydney and Kimberly go a few more rounds at the office.

SYDNEY: Look who's here—America's favorite homicidal maniac.

KIMBERLY: Park it, Sydney. Is Peter here?

SYDNEY: No, he's not. Have you tried Amanda's? I hear they've been spending a lot of time together lately. Oh, but you can't go there, can you? Your little Mickey Mouse watch'll start screaming. How do you ever find things to accessorize with that, anyway?

KIMBERLY: You're a lying little bitch.

SYDNEY: Not this time, kookie-bird.

The nurse suggests Amanda talk to Jack about the good times to revive him from his coma.

AMANDA: It's me, Jack, Amanda. I was just thinking about some of our special times we had together. Like the time I forgot to fold your socks and you pounded my face into the bedpost. I needed eighteen stitches that time. Or remember when you broke my hand because I wore the wrong color dress? I remember how I cried all night. Remember this, Jack, for every black eye and bruise you ever gave me, you son of a bitch, I hope you die.

Amanda's mad to find Peter in her bed after she got drunk and seduced him. So the morning after she rails at him.

AMANDA: I'm on the edge, Peter. It's hard work wishing Jack dead full time.

Richard doesn't understand why Jane objects to Jo going to work in Hawaii with them.

RICHARD: For what, Jane? So you could take me someplace romantic to tell me you don't really love me?

And Jake's not happy when Jane tells him Jo and Richard are going to Hawaii without her.

JANE: I'm sure they'll get a lot done. Between the coconut oil massages and the double Mai Tais.

JAKE: How could she do this?

JANE: Welcome to the Friends of Jo club. Any damn fool can join.

Sydney has Amanda on tape telling Peter she'll kill Jack if he revives. Michael wants her to throw it out.

MICHAEL: Syd, everything in life isn't about exploitation and betrayal.

SYDNEY: What are you, nuts? Of course it is.

MICHAEL: You never change.

Jane's having a party and Sydney, on work release from "confessing" to running down Michael, is there.

SYDNEY: I'm a designer, too, you know. I'm not just working for Jane to satisfy some silly court order probation.

AMANDA: And to think your talent might have been wasted making license plates in some women's prison.

Jake invites Amanda to lunch to get some investment advice about his F.B.I. windfall.

AMANDA: Ooh, I didn't realize it was so late.

JAKE: Late? You just got here.

AMANDA: Well, I figured lunch wouldn't go well, so I scheduled a one o'clock meeting.

Amanda demurs when Michael insists she could persuade Peter to reinstate him at the hospital.

MICHAEL: Well, Amanda, you and I both know that you could get a Tibetan monk to strip naked and dance the hootchie-kootchie if you wanted to bad enough, or if there was something in it for you.

Alison is amazed at how many "friends" pack Amanda's first party as owner of the complex.

ALISON: I never really pictured Amanda as the social butterfly type. Social moth, maybe, black widow, really.

Dirt, Skirts, and Flirts

M*elrose Place* hit its stride as the second season began, hooking fans with an intricate spell of passion, intrigue, and double-crossing. The show became more like a typical soap opera, with plots more densely interwoven, multiplying the lunacy. A lion's share of the credit for the startling turnaround belonged to Heather Locklear. Her devilish Amanda Woodward spiced up plotlines like a shot of Tabasco in a Bloody Mary.

AMANDARRIFIC

Amanda's first official act as landlady of the apartment complex was to throw a poolside shindig for one and all. Well, *almost* all. Alison got detention, and spent the night chained to her office desk. That gave Amanda unfettered access to Billy, who cheerfully fetched refreshments and unseated Matt as lamest white boy on the dance floor.

Amanda's hunk-itch knew no limits, which especially unnerved Jo. As soon as Jake's rippling muscles caught Ms. Woodward's eye, she had him rearranging all her major appliances. Jo sighed and went back to the darkroom.

Amanda's touch wasn't always golden, however. Hiring Ted Ryan as the Peeping-Tom-building-manager was a major boo-boo. By the time he'd drilled holes into half the women's closet walls, spied on Amanda and Jake doing a samba between the sheets, and stashed himself away in the complex's attic, Amanda was fit to be tied. Or rather, fit *to* tie. She and Jo wrapped Teddy up like a fly in a spider's web and taunted him with a knife. But Amanda decided to stay on the safe side of the law, and refrained from gouging his eyes out. Ted got the message and vamoosed.

MAMA MIA

When Jo drafted preteen model Sarah Owens from the Models, Inc. agency, which just *happened* to be headed by Amanda's estranged mom, Hillary Michaels, the fur flew. These two hadn't cozied up for a mother

25

"Special Guest Star" Heather Locklear: "The whole show is evil!"

and child chat for years, and Amanda wanted to keep it that way. But when head honcho Bruce insisted D&D use the agency, mommy dearest was back in her daughter's life.

Amanda's hackles rose even higher when she got an eyeful of her mom's slimy boy-toy, Chas Russell. The smarmy young Casanova leered at Amanda every time Hillary's back was turned. Yet, in typical *Melrose* fashion, Amanda forged ahead and gave him the plum job of assisting the perennially overworked Alison. Other than wowing Bruce by instituting a weekly after-hours poker game, Chas left the grunt work to Alison and concentrated all his lecherous energies on Amanda. The cad soon had her in his sleazy clutches. Alison witnessed their interoffice liplock just as she was about to grumble to Amanda that her advertising wonder-boy was a flop. But there was no catching the boss's ear while Chas had her mouth working overtime.

Instead, a repulsed Alison lost no time squealing the news to Billy. The trusty *Melrose* gossip daisy chain sprang into action. Billy blabbed to Jake. Jake squawked at Amanda. Amanda chewed out Alison for opening up her big yap.

Meanwhile, Chas was kicked out on his behind when Amanda regained her senses and rebuffed his further advances. Quicker than a rat runs up a drainpipe, he slapped D&D with a $10 million sexual harassment suit. Bruce pushed for a quick and quiet settlement, but instead, Amanda marched into the hearing with her head high and her skirt hem even higher.

Girl Scout Alison couldn't tell a lie, and recounted the story of the smooch to the drooling committee. But scumbucket Chas celebrated his victory a tad too soon. Hillary caught on to his scam, raced to her daughter's defense, and the case was thrown out. Sure that this would bury the family hatchet, Hillary was stunned that Amanda still rejected her. Hillary had no choice but to spin off onto her own show, *Models Inc.*

ALISON THROUGH THE LOOKING GLASS

Alison Parker's life took more twists and turns than a roller coaster. Her beau of the first season, Keith, lost all his appeal when he morphed into a psychotic lunatic obsessed with having her all to himself. His fatal attraction began to simmer when Alison left him—and Seattle—to return to L.A. It started to boil when he saw that she and Billy were playing on the same team again.

Alone at the office, Alison was spooked by another nasty phone call, never suspecting her buddy Keith was the dialer. In fact, when he popped up moments later in the dark, empty D&D hallway, Alison clung to him. In no time, he had her drowning her fears in a snootful of martinis.

Keith's lunacy escalated when he bashed his head into the television set at his hotel room, then reported to the police that the stalker had used the "same tire iron" to hit him that had been used on Billy months before. That was enough to set off Billy's bullshit radar—he knew he never said a thing about a tire iron to the cops after he was attacked earlier.

Alison continued to ignore the warning signs flashing at her louder than a bad AM station. She resisted Keith's pleas that she return with him to Seattle, but, what the hell, she agreed to give him a lift to the airport for a fond farewell. By the time she toodled over to his house, Keith was in full psycho rage. When he lunged at Alison, she *finally* got the message that the guy was out of his mind. Summoning up karate skills she'd kept under wraps previously, Alison doubled him up with one swift kick to his groin and got the hell out.

The L.A.P.D., who must have been running low on coffee, bought Keith's cuckoo story that *Alison* had attacked *him*. Depressed once more, Alison eased down into a bottle of vodka to smooth out the rough spots.

CAMPBELL'S SOUP

Billy's idea of seeking justice—not that Alison had asked him to—was to wing up to Seattle to settle the score himself. He immediately set about bending laws right and left as he tried to locate Keith and rearrange his face. Breaking and entering, assault and battery (with Keith's coworkers as witnesses)—the eager Lancelot charged ahead. Alison later found out that Keith had killed himself. Billy learned that he'd accrued some much-needed frequent flyer miles.

Back at D&D, Amanda continued to heap projects onto Alison's plate, who proceeded to crack further under the strain. In an attempt to smooth matters over, Billy came on to Amanda (although why he thought that would make Alison *happy* instead of *miserable* was unclear). Alison's reaction was to keep on working toward her Ph.D. in alcohol consumption.

Billy and Alison did enjoy—in their own bickering way—a brief frolic at the fancy digs of Steve Bryant, a luxury hotel owner. Though Billy's editor, Nancy Donner, had warned him to go alone to the weekend interview, Alison faked being sick to tag along with him, anyway. Arielle, Steve's Lolita of a daughter, flirted with Billy, which irked Alison. When Daddy-O figured out Billy had company with him, contrary to his editor's orders, Campbell's bashfully direct confession won the day. He and Alison were invited to stay and enjoy themselves.

Following that short idyll, Alison bagged a rich new client, Steve McMillan, a computer bigwig. Of course, a green-eyed Billy fumed throughout a horse-filled weekend at Steve's ranch. He didn't even notice that Steve had set his sights on Jo, anyway. But that little romance quickly evaporated, with a confused and envious Alison nudging her gal pal out of the picture.

A peek into Alison's office e-mail, where a suggestive message from Steve blinked unanswered, fueled Billy's fears. Alison hemmed and hawed about whether to return Steve's affections. By the time she'd decided a rich boyfriend might be just the ticket, it was too late. Steve had tired of playing the Alison-Waiting-Game and zipped off to Paris to start a new computer venture.

Amanda acted fast and scooped up Billy for a passionate fling before he could get back together with Alison. Billy discovered that two girls are better than one. Between Amanda's lustiness and Alison's companionship, he was a happy-happy boy-boy.

Meanwhile, Celia Morales, a flirtatious colleague of his from *Escapade* magazine, moved in with Billy and Alison during fumigation of her condo. Quarters were tight, which, of course, sent Alison into maximum grousing mode. She grudgingly pitched in to edit a piece Billy and Celia cowrote. It turned out so well, their boss Nancy pitted them against one another to compete for a promotion.

The bittersweet victory was Billy's—he got the promotion, but the job was in New York City. Alison resisted his suggestion that she move with him, so he struck out for the Big Apple solo. Many disappointing rounds of phone tag ensued, and when the two did speak, their chats fell flat. Fearing that a long-distance relationship would never work, Alison cashed in her frequent flyer miles and surprised Billy at his apartment. And, boy, was he surprised! Alison found him there with a shapely model, Andrea. The sight was enough to send Alison's feverish imagination into overdrive. She took off in a huff.

After tracking Alison down, Billy assured her that Andrea's visit was harmless. But in his enthusiasm, he leaped to the conclusion that Alison was ready to join him in Manhattan. Not so. More accusations and frustrations filled the air, and Alison jetted back to L.A., convinced they had no future. On the plane, the cocktail cart looked mighty appealing.

Determined not to lose her, Billy chucked his fancy new job, grabbed a shlocky ring from a knock-off street vendor and rushed back to pop

He just plays one on T.V.: Doug Savant and Courtney Thorne-Smith at Aaron Spelling's Christmas party, 1994.

the question. Jane hoodwinked a dolled-up Alison into going to a fancy restaurant, and our Romeo took it from there. From shmaltzy piano music in the background, to the ring nestled at the bottom of her champagne flute, to a flowery proposal on bended knee, Billy wooed Alison for all he was worth. Ever the modern girl, she held him off until the next day, when she accepted over hot dogs in the park, her treat.

The newly engaged Billy blanched every time Amanda wiggled over to Alison and dropped blatant hints that Mr. Fiancé wasn't the paragon he pretended to be. Amanda swore up and down to Billy that she'd zip her lip about their juicy fling, but she immediately blabbed to a none-too-amused Jake.

Mayhem broke out at the Shooters engagement party when a furious Jake—Billy's best man, no less—belted him right in the kisser over Amanda. Billy sweated through a long night worrying if Alison would forgive and forget. By morning she was all smiles, assuring him that her fling with Steve McMillan was every bit as wanton as his frolic with Amanda.

SHE CAN'T GO HOME AGAIN

Alison and Billy flew to Wisconsin for her father's fiftieth birthday celebration. To Billy's amazement, she had not told her parents about their engagement. At the birthday bash, he grabbed the mike from Adam, an old boyfriend of Alison's who was waxing nostalgic to the crowd about their high school romance, and delivered the happy news of their upcoming wedding. The reserved reception to his announcement puzzled him.

The eerie atmosphere at Casa Parker grew as Billy watched Alison recoil in horror at a childhood train set and doll he'd dragged up from the family basement. A feverish nightmare starring those same toys convinced both of them something mysterious, deep, and difficult was bothering Alison. After they returned to L.A., Alison started therapy to try to figure out why bad dreams were plaguing her. Billy, true to form, was resentful of Alison's therapist, and kept trying to convince her that he was all the help she needed. The good doctor's amorous advances toward her didn't help the situation.

MANCINI MISERIES

The Mancini divorce continued on its downward spiral. Determined to start life anew, Jane put on a brave face and partied with Alison, Amanda, and Jo. Her bold front crumbled when she became physically ill at the sight of her two-timing husband out with his doctor doll, Kimberly.

Amanda suggested she get some bottom-line satisfaction, so Jane switched lawyers and called off the nice 'n easy no-fault divorce. Now it's gloves off, she ordered her mouthpiece; let's grab a piece of his future earnings.

MY SISTER SYDNEY

Jane's little sister Sydney blew in from the Windy City to cheer up her sib. But rather than offer tea and sympathy, Sydney set her redheaded-sights on her soon-to-be ex-brother-in-law. Not that Michael noticed her loopy plays—he was too busy jumping Kimberly's bones while plotting to deny their affair during the divorce proceedings. Kimberly caught a whiff of her competition, though, and warned the small-time vamp to steer clear.

Jane turned to old friend Sam Towler for the kindness and support Sydney had no time to offer. He was sweet and considerate, but too much the gentleman to take advantage of Jane in her vulnerable state.

Jane, that innocent little lamb, sputtered in disbelief when Michael calmly told lie upon lie on the witness stand. Kimberly was more concerned with protecting her career than being nabbed for perjury, and she crumbled on cross examination. Michael ranted and raved at his plan gone awry.

> "I like *Melrose Place* because it's similar to another nighttime serial which I loved—*Dynasty*. The characters on *Melrose* are deceitful and three-dimensional. I really enjoy Kimberly—she makes the show for me. She's so spontaneous!"
> —Shawn Harrison
> (Waldo Faldo, *Family Matters*)

In a characteristic display of bad taste, Michael threw himself a stag party to celebrate the final divorce decree. Well, it was almost stag—Amanda managed to attend. The rest of the women rallied around Jane.

Kimberly was called out of town, and Sydney rushed to Michael's side. He was happy to indulge in a roll in the hay, but Syd read meaning into their steamy encounter that just wasn't there. Never one to mince words, Michael dumped her. A crushed Sydney realized she was nothing more than a moment's diversion to Michael as she watched him beg Kimberly not to move away from L.A.

DESIGNATED DRUNK DRIVER

Determined to hold onto Kimberly, Michael whisked her off for an elegant night on the town. They drank themselves into a happy stupor during the sumptuous meal. Afterwards, a tanked Michael slid behind the wheel and off the two zoomed into the night. The booze bolstered his courage, and he blurted out a proposal. Kimberly instantly accepted. It

Daphne Zuniga

LADY WITH A LENS

Daphne Zuniga clambered onto *Melrose Place* with a mission to accomplish. Her gritty, sharp-tongued character, Jo Reynolds, was created to fill the black hole left by Sandy Harling, the southern-fried waitress/actress who said sayonara midway through the first season. From the get-go, Jo's smoldering, dark-haired beauty stood apart from the sunny California cuties surrounding the pool.

As Zuniga told *Rolling Stone*: "Maybe *Melrose Place* is the thinking person's nighttime soap. You could say we're also equal-opportunity beefcake and cheesecake. If you like blondes, we've *got* blondes. You happen to want brunettes, we've *got* brunettes. And if you feel like a redhead, *boy*, do we have a redhead for you. We've got girls; we've got guys, too. We've got it all here at *Melrose Place*."

It's not surprising that Zuniga is able to wax philosophical about her work; she's the daughter of a Unitarian minister-mother and a philosophy professor-father. Raised to look beyond the often flimsy worlds of entertainment, Zuniga's actively committed to numerous political causes, like the Committee in Solidarity with the People of El Salvador (Zuniga has a special affinity for that group, since she has family in Guatemala), the Environmental Communications Office, and Young Artists United (she's a founding member), which seeks to help kids over the hurdles of becoming adults.

When it comes to work, Zuniga's résumé has enough heft to scare Mike Tyson. Raised in the San Francisco Bay area, she spent a year at the prestigious American Conservatory Theater (fellow alums include Annette Bening). She also completed the rigorous three-year theater program at U.C.L.A. After college, Zuniga continued to train, eventually completing four years of private acting preparation, and a stint at the Loft Studio under the instruction of coach Peggy Feury.

Zuniga's auspicious TV movie debut was in the 1983 CBS movie, *Quarterback Princess*, which starred Helen Hunt (of *Mad About You*). A two-episode appearance on *Family Ties* followed soon after, as one of the wonky girlfriends of Alex Keaton (Michael J. Fox).

On the big screen, Zuniga showed up in a number of unmemorable parts, but broke through in 1985's *The Sure Thing*. Her straitlaced character, Alison Bradbury, drove cross-country with Gib, portrayed by a then-seventeen-year-old John Cusack. The pair bickered their way across America; she planned to meet up with her stuffy boyfriend (Boyd Gaines) and he was anxious to hook up a "sure thing" in the luscious form of Nicollette Sheridan (her film debut). Of course, by the movie's end, Gib and Alison were in love—good preparation for the love quadrangles that stud *Melrose Place*.

The success of *The Sure Thing* boosted Zuniga's career, but, in narrow-minded Hollywood fashion, all the scripts that followed called for her to play more downright uptight grinds. To escape the stereotype, she opted instead to do *The Stone Pillow*, a television project in which she costarred as a naive social worker whose eyes are opened by a bag lady, played by Lucille Ball.

Zuniga skipped back to the big screen as Princess Vespa in Mel Brooks's 1987 spoof *Spaceballs* (as a futuristic Jewish-American princess) and then earned good notices in 1989 for *The Fly II* with costar Eric Stoltz. Also in an attempt to broaden her image, Zuniga played a sexy Latin dancer who beds a priest (played by Tom Berenger) in 1988's *Last Rites*. "I was terrified," she told *Mademoiselle*, "yet I knew I should do it."

Like fellow cast members Grant Show and Courtney Thorne-Smith, *Melrose* came along after a dry spell in Zuniga's career. Darren Star, the show's creator, writer, and executive producer, called on his former U.C.L.A. roomie to spice up his show with her distinctive presence and voice. And she's come through for him, though she might be loathe to admit it. As she commented to *Entertainment Weekly* "[My] self-assured part comes in waves, comes and goes. I think too much."

But Zuniga is savvy enough to appreciate *Melrose's* considerable charms. The money she's paid to juice up Jo recently bought her a house. She also commanded a starring role in a 1995 NBC movie, *Degree of Guilt*. And she's now intimately acquainted with just about every shade of black clothing known to man.

Asked if she would live amid the madness of *Melrose*, however, Daphne laughingly told *TV Guide*, "Honestly? I'd last a week. Maybe two. And then I would just bite the deposit and leave. Because if this were real life, I'd probably have lawsuits on my hands for beating up Amanda and that little tart Sydney."

was a joyful, but brief, period of engagement. Michael was so blotto that he lost control of the car and it crashed off a bridge.

At the emergency room, a comatose Kimberly was wheeled away, while Michael was merely paralyzed. Luckily, his manipulative faculties were fully functioning. Fearing legal repercussions if his high blood alcohol level was revealed, he browbeat Matt into monkeying around with the hospital lab results. Although Matt did as he was asked—when has he ever refused Michael?—the pair continued to fight over the tampered files.

Amid the turmoil, Kimberly's mother Marion berated Michael for ruining her daughter's life. She then whisked the comatose doc home to Ohio.

Michael panicked when news came from Cincinnati that Kimberly had not survived her injuries. Matt attempted to help by getting Michael placed in a rehab center where he could learn to use his legs again. His stay there was brief, though, since Michael was able to bamboozle Jane into letting him recuperate at her apartment.

Jane was determined that her ex-husband's grumpy presence wouldn't interrupt her new, independent life. She blithely necked poolside with her legal eagle, Robert, while a seething Michael watched. The sideshow got his legs twitching. Michael dragged himself out of bed, only to fall and be rescued by good samaritan Sydney.

THE DOCTOR IS IN . . . AND OUT

Sydney had been keeping busy since Michael dumped her. Drawn into the world of high-priced hooking by a chic madam named Lauren, Syd nevertheless annoyed her "dates" with her endless chitchat. Michael, of all people, bailed her out when she got picked up on prostitution charges.

As a payback, Michael lured Sydney into getting a hooker friend to seduce Jane's beau, Robert. By taping the whole nasty episode, Michael planned to wreak maximum torment on his ex-wife with undeniable proof that her white knight was just another blackhearted knave. Jane shrieked in horror as the erotic drama played back on her TV. Sydney soon crumbled and confessed her role after Michael gave her the cold shoulder once again. Jane exacted revenge on Michael by tossing him out of her apartment, and flinging his cane into the pool for good measure.

An unrepentant Michael swallowed his woes with painkillers. After he harassed Jane once too often on the phone, Robert got Jane a restraining order to keep Michael a safe distance away. Certain she wouldn't have the guts to use it, Michael nonchalantly rang her doorbell. Jane dialed 9–1–1, lickety-split. Before the police arrived, Sydney grabbed Michael, stowed him in her apartment, and even began scamming pills for him.

Back at his beach house, Michael fell into a drugged stupor. A crafty Sydney caught the woozy doc mumbling about Matt's tinkering with the hospital records. Sydney instantly had a new profession—blackmail.

Determined to tether Michael into holy matrimony, Syd got the maitre d' from the restaurant to tell Michael that he remembered how snookered Mikey had been the night of the accident. Quicker than a wink, Syd moved herself into his beach house and ran up the doc's credit cards redecorating their "love nest." She haunted the hospital corridors chatting up his colleagues, introducing herself as the girlfriend who'd gotten him off painkillers and over his dead fiancée. Back on the job, a startled Dr. Mancini was called out of surgery to the telephone. It was Sydney saying, don't forget, darling, our wedding's next week.

With the happy day fast approaching, Sydney and Jane's mother Katherine came to town with a family heirloom gown for the bride. Jane became so enraged at the sight of her devious little sister in the dress that she shoved her into the pool—veil and all. Syd eventually got her way, though. She and a morose Michael tied their lonely knot on the beach.

Jane's wedding gift was a lovely framed, signed confession from Matt, admitting to tampering with the hospital's blood alcohol records. To add to her amusement about the gift, Jane promised the happy couple she would hotfoot it to the cops with a copy if either Michael or Sydney ever bothered her again.

After the marriage, Michael planned to do away with his blackmailing bride while on their honeymoon. Knowing how Michael felt about Sydney, Matt trailed them, but could have saved himself the time and worry. Michael was actually beginning to fall for his wily wife.

The sisters, however, continued their spat when dear old granny kicked off and left a nice chunk of change to Jane. But two problems loomed: first, she left the dough to Jane *and Michael*; second, Michael was now married to Sydney. Jane was so anxious to launch her own company, however, that she took mini-mogul Amanda's advice and gave her ex a one-half silent partnership to finance the venture.

For a moment, everyone was happy—at least a little bit. Jane got the business, Sydney got the ring, and Michael got laid.

SHE'S ALIVE

Who should stumble into this cozy scene but Kimberly, alive and wearing the same dress in which she was almost killed? At the sight of his not-quite-dead fiancée, Michael attempted to unload wifey. But Syd played her blackmail card again and threatened to call in the law to question Michael. Unfortunately, Sydney's victory was short-lived; a smitten Michael scurried off with Kimberly for a night of torrid sex.

Complaining of vicious headaches, Kimberly sometime later slipped from the rumpled sheets and stood before the bathroom mirror. To the revulsion of *Melrose* fans everywhere, she peeled off a wig and revealed a huge scar tracking the side of her head like the Great Wall of China.

When Sydney rubbed Kimberly's face in the fact that Syd's name was the one on the Mancini marriage license, Kimberly twisted Syd's arm into a tight pretzel. The bruised Mancini missus got no sympathy from her indifferent husband, who practically ran her over zooming back to Kimberly at the beach house.

But the woman awaiting him at home was seething with rage. How could he forget her so fast? How could he marry That Tart? Michael fumbled for answers and swore it was all going to change. Kimberly then flip-flopped again. In a personality switcheroo, she vamped him in satin lingerie under her doctor's coat while on-duty at the hospital.

Foolish pride on both sides prevented Syd and Jane from comforting one another. It was a sad moment for sisterhood as each of them stood crying on opposite sides of Jane's apartment door. Sliding back into her old habits, Sydney was reduced to working as a stripper. Unfortunately, at her first appearance as "Jungle Jane," at the Body Stocking, the entire *Melrose* male contingent trooped in to celebrate Billy's farewell to bachelorhood. In utter shame, Syd fled the stage.

Madam Lauren refused to rehire Syd and threatened trouble if she didn't make good on the $15,000 still owed. Syd slowly stumbled from stripper to streetwalker. Clearly an amateur, she was attacked by the more experienced girls on the block and ended up in the emergency room under the care of none other than Dr. Kimberly Shaw. She would have been better off back on Hollywood Boulevard. As far as we know, Lauren's still waiting on that fifteen grand.

UNEASY RIDERS

Love's course ran smoother for Jake and Jo when they decided to hang their toothbrushes in the same holder. Though Amanda lured Jake with an offer to appear in an ad for Red Sage Beer, he stuck with his bike shop.

Jake's business sense failed him completely when he overbid on a pile of dilapidated clunkers. Figuring he'd recoup the loss by fixing them up for resale, he grabbed the nearest monkey wrench and got to work. Amanda sashayed over to the shop and broke his concentration. Enticed

Couples We'd Like to See

·····························

Melrose is a festival of pairings, un-pairings, re-pairings. Yikes, our heads are spinning from the ever-shifting romantic tornado whizzing by week after week. Here are our candidates for some fresh, new duos.

Michael and Matt
These two don't make a move without consulting each other. It's high time they recognized how deep their bond goes.

Billy and Sydney
Don't laugh. These two share a refreshing innocence that sets them apart from their jaded neighbors. Throw in their innate passionate temperaments, and watch the fur fly.

Kimberly and Sydney
It has to happen. But who'll play Butch and who'll play Femme?

Kimberly and Peter
These reformed, sophisticated villains would have a hot time licking each other's wounds. Throw in a few bandages and they'll be feeling fine by morning.

Hayley and Brooke
If only we'd all looked the other way and given her one fabulous night to get it out of her system. But it's too late now, Daddy-O.

Amanda and Richie Sambora
We don't know what it is—there's just something about him that seems *perfect* for our little Amanda.

into taking a quick break with her, Jake left a blowtorch aflame as they scurried out. Somehow Amanda managed to knock the lit torch over—*without either of them noticing*. The greasy shop exploded in flames.

Jo discovered the blaze and ran in, screaming for Jake. The shop was a melted mess, with no insurance money to come once the adjustor figured out how the fire had started. Jo and Jake argued about the whole crazy incident, and he put the kibosh on their romance since she didn't trust him. In frustration, he attacked the refrigerator, which terrified Jo, who nevertheless cried and begged him to stay.

Amanda plucked up the available hunk and bedded him down. Life under the covers was fabulous, but Jake was uneasy about the cushy job Amanda's father Palmer had offered him. He took it, though, and in no time was confiding to Amanda that Daddy's vintage auto reproduction business kept phony books.

Palmer suspected Jake had figured out the deal was a dud, but completely believed Jake's Alfred E. Neuman "what, me worry?" imitation. The F.B.I. soon fumbled onto the scene. Their subtle recommendation that Jake squeal rather than be charged as an accessory convinced him to sing like a birdy. Palmer's scheme was exposed and all hell broke loose.

Out of familial loyalty, Amanda sided with her father and kicked Jake out. He wandered down to Shooters in a funk, and found Jo there playing pool with the guys. Twinges of regret shot through him like needles in a pin cushion.

Amanda watched helplessly as dear old dad was hauled off to jail. The situation went from bad to worse when Palmer jumped bail and skipped town. Figuring he'd contact his daughter, the F.B.I. kept close tabs on Amanda. Her boss Bruce suggested a little R&R where the feds wouldn't tail her. She gratefully jetted off to Hawaii—what, no F.B.I. branch there?—for sun and solitude.

No sooner had she filled her pail with sand than Amanda learned that Alison had snatched away her prized "Mountain Tog" account. Before happy hour had begun, Amanda stomped out of paradise and back to the office. Alison's killer instinct turned out to be harmless, and she sheepishly relinquished control of the account to Amanda. The thinly-veiled threat of reprisal hovered over Alison, much to Amanda's pleasure.

SAILOR BOY

Jo rediscovered an old boyfriend, Reed Carter, at her high school reunion. He laid on her a lame story of woe about an unfair drug rap that had kept him in the clink. Somehow Jo found this creep appealing and soon she was joining him for jaunts aboard his snazzy boat, *The Pretty Lady*. Despite Reed's bizarre fondness for weapons—he opened fire on a cat slinking nearby when he heard a noise on deck—Jo fell into his loving arms. But when she stumbled across a suspicious locked compartment, her antenna for trouble shot up.

Reed asked Jo to hold onto a suitcase of his for safekeeping. She, of course, immediately took a peek—only clothes, pictures, and other personal effects. This gave Reed the chance to berate her for violating his trust—gee, hadn't she heard that song before from Jake? But soon after, Jo overheard Reed's midnight upperdeck rendezvous. The next morning she spied the stash of drugs in the secret compartment. When Reed realized she was on to him, he taped her mouth—ouch—and locked her in the hold with the drugs.

Jo kicked her way out of the bolted chamber and the two scuffled on deck, a battle royale complete with harpoons. She managed to pitch Reed overboard, but he climbed back up and rushed at her with a flare gun. Jo shot him dead, and the Coast Guard showed up the next morning and arrested her for murder.

After calling Jake for help, Jo cooled her heels in jail. Amanda refused to post bail, fearing she'd be connected to Reed's illegal venture because he had gotten her to invest in his "business." Jo's troubles worsened when her public defender, Benjamin Skyler, urged her to cut a deal as an accomplice. No one believed she would be sleeping with Reed without being part of his drug dealing. She wailed her innocence to the P.D., the D.A., and anyone else with official initials.

Billy and Alison showed up with cash advanced on their credit cards, but the D.A. fought against bail. At the last moment Amanda felt a twinge of responsibility, and wiggled in with superlawyer Walter Kovaks. A few short hearings later, Kovaks had gotten the charges dismissed.

Jo was a free woman. Well, not really. Jo was a young, single, pregnant woman. And not so dearly departed Reed was the daddy. She still attracted men, however. Jo found time to indulge in a quick fling with a new buddy, Gregory Davis, who didn't suspect her maternal condition.

Meanwhile, during photo shoots, young model Sarah Owens began dropping hints about her abusive boyfriend Hank, who wanted her to leave the L.A. high life and return to Iowa with him. Jo offered sympathetic support when Sarah showed up bruised and shaken at the apartment complex. Soon Hank was pounding down the door. After yelling back and forth, he lashed out at Jo and shoved her down the stairs.

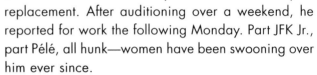

Andrew Shue

IF THE SHUE FITS

I t's nearly impossible to imagine *Melrose Place* without Andrew Shue's version of wonder-boy Billy Campbell. But many viewers don't realize that Shue was not the first choice for the original ensemble. It was only when the newcomer originally hired to play the part, Canadian actor Stephen Fanning, failed to hit the right notes with producers and directors that Shue was hastily hired as an early-on replacement. After auditioning over a weekend, he reported for work the following Monday. Part JFK Jr., part Pélé, all hunk—women have been swooning over him ever since.

Such twists seem to sweep up Shue at every turn. Probably the least "actorish" of all his *Melrose* colleagues, Shue appears to move through the world with the assurance of a well-seasoned winner. From his earliest days as a soccer player in the comfortable New Jersey suburb of South Orange, Shue has excelled. In fact, he was the kind of high school superachiever who probably caused parents to nudge their kids and hiss, "Why can't you be more like *him*?"

Perhaps the fact that his father once ran for congress spurred Shue's interest in public service. In any event, the future actor's college applications were a guidance counselor's dream—he was elected student body president, senior class president, and student commencement speaker at his high school graduation.

One early goal that eluded Shue's golden-boy grasp was acceptance to Harvard. He put the defeat in perspective, though, and attended another Ivy League institution, Dartmouth College in Hanover, New Hampshire (nothing to sneeze at!). There, Shue spent four years duplicating the success he'd found in high school. He led Dartmouth to a soccer league championship. Personally, his hard work won him an all-Ivy ranking, four-times over.

In the classroom, Shue studied history, although he toyed with being a lawyer (as well as architect, Secret Service agent, and sports reporter). Dartmouth was obviously a defining period in Shue's life—his ties to college pals remain so strong that until his recent marriage to Jennifer Hageney, he lived with two fellow alums.

After graduation in 1989, Shue grabbed at the only opportunity available to go pro in soccer—in Zimbabwe, Africa. Although he had to juggle working full-time as a high school geometry teacher (and soccer coach), Shue was able to fulfill a lifetime dream of playing professionally, before screaming crowds as large as 70,000 as a member of the Bulawayo Highlanders team.

A career as a performer may never have crossed Shue's busy mind if it hadn't been for his sister, actress Elisabeth (*Soapdish, Leaving Las Vegas*) Shue. She had spotted her brother's star power when she made him the star of super-8 home movie extravaganzas. But it was only when Elisabeth told a friend that her brother was an actor that her sib actually considered the idea.

It wasn't long before Shue walked into Aaron Spelling and Fox Television's line of sight. He was cast in a pilot of *Gulf City*, an action-adventure series shot in Florida. Luckily for Shue, that pilot sank just as *Melrose Place* began filming its premiere episode.

As *Melrose* has evolved into a seething den of lust and power-grabbing, Shue has found himself on the receiving end of many an on-air smooch. "I don't mind doing one love scene every now and then," he remarked philosophically to *Vanity Fair*, "but I don't like doing a lot of them."

And while he beds almost as many babes as Jake, Billy remains one of the show's sweeter characters. But don't be fooled, warns Shue. "For everyone who thinks Billy is clueless, here's a clue. He knows everything that's going on," he assured *Entertainment Weekly*.

Off-camera, Shue sprints around as though he's in a permanent race for student body president. One summer hiatus he returned to South Orange, where he directed the Cougar Soccer Camp for local kids. He's now a spokesman for the World Cup, and even published a daily newspaper during the 1994 tournament.

As cofounder of Do Something, a youth-oriented community service organization, Shue continues his goal of motivating others to participate in improving the world around them. Like Students Serving Seniors, a program he created in high school to match energetic youths with seniors in need of assistance, Do Something satisfies the actor's genuine urge to make the world a better place. But don't think the guy's a complete stick-in-the-mud—after all, he can touch his nose with his tongue.

Jo survived the spill still pregnant, and recuperated at the hospital with Jake attentively watching over her, to Amanda's irritation.

FROM RUSSIA WITH LOVE

The strangest marriage on *Melrose*—or one of them, anyway—involved Matt Fielding. Yes, Matt, the gay guy of the apartment complex. While working at the hospital, courtesy of Michael's influence, Matt met Dr. Katya Petrova, a Russian doctor looking to stay in America. Seeing Matt as a safe haven, she proposed by waving a wad of cash to cushion the deal. The old softie passed on the bucks, but couldn't refuse Katya's request, especially after meeting her darling daughter Nikki.

Trouble started to brew immediately when the I.N.S. began investigating the newlyweds. Soon Matt and Katya were buried under mountains of red tape and bureaucratic interviews. *And* it began to dawn on Matt that being married—pretend or not—was going to put a serious crimp in his dating style.

A family illness back in Russia forced Katya to return to her homeland, though little Nikki remained with Matt. When it turned out Katya wouldn't be coming back to L.A., Matt learned how it felt to have a female break his heart as he bid a sad good-bye to his stepdaughter.

Time heals all wounds, though. Soon Matt had fallen for Jeffrey Lindley, a coy charmer. After some false starts, Matt learned Jeff's secret—he was a navy officer who was still in the closet. When Matt sauntered up to the navy base unexpectedly, Jeff was alarmed and ordered him to leave, pronto. Later at the hospital, the boys hashed it out and agreed to start over. Matt persisted in urging Jeff to come out to his parents and fellow officers. Finally he did, and in the blink of an eye he was shipped back east without his commission. Thank you, Matt.

A VIEW TO A KILL

Thoroughly disgusted (for some unknown reason) with Dr. Mancini, by now Kimberly had switched gears and was plotting to bring him down. First she removed the "no penicillin—allergic" warning from Michael's patient's chart. After the unlucky patient suffered a seizure, Michael was brought up on negligence charges and lost the chief residency spot. Next, Kimberly tried to hire a hit man to kill Michael for $5,000, but the thug scoffed at her meager offer.

Ultimately, Kimberly decided her grand scheme required Sydney's assistance. Taking advantage of the bruised woman's desperation, she lured Syd into her web. How could they murder Michael? Let us count the ways.

The pair's first attempt involved drugging Michael with a dose of sleeping pills slipped into his beer. Once he drifted off into a deep haze they dragged him out to the car, which was already conveniently running and filling the garage with lethal fumes. But that killjoy, Jane, arrived to rebuke her ex-hubby for missing a meeting and discovered his slumped body before he was sufficiently cold. A girl's gotta do what a girl's gotta do—so Jane opened the garage doors and revived him with mouth-to-mouth resuscitation. Michael later let her know how much he enjoyed it, the letch.

Determined to mow him down, Kimberly hatched a more complicated scheme. Donning a short blonde wig, she stole Jane's car and paged Michael at the hospital with an emergency message to meet "Jane." Michael slinked into plain sight and Kimberly merrily plowed into him. As he lay motionless in intensive care, ex-Mrs. Mancini number one was arrested for attempted murder.

WEDDING BELL BLUES

Billy and Alison's plans were further muddled when big sister Meredith refused to hop the shuttle from San Francisco for the impending nuptials. Alison's dad John was quick to blame her absence on drugs; Mom's mouth was set in a permanent grimace.

Moments before the ceremony was to begin, an already unsettled Alison freaked out when her father whispered to her not to cry. In that instant, Alison realized that the horror gripping her was the memory of her father's sexual abuse. When she was a helpless child he would murmur the pervert's mantra—"Don't tell"—as he groped her in the basement. Never one to be cunning when unthinking honesty would do, Alison stammered that she remembered what he had done to her. Dad didn't take it too well—he threatened bodily harm if she ever divulged his nasty little habit. Alison did what any sensible person would do—she bolted right out the window, without a word to her waiting groom.

Up at Meredith's San Francisco digs, the sisters dithered about what to do. Feisty Alison had trouble understanding the depths of Meredith's fears about coming face to face with their father. Little did they realize how soon that confrontation would take place—the old man was parked outside, spying on them.

Come and Gone

Who played that flipped-out handyman drilling holes in all the closets? Wasn't that Amanda's boss on *90210* last night? We could swear that was Jake's mom starring on Broadway in *Nine*. Here's the scoop on characters we've loved and lost.

AMY LOCANE

Hi, Y'All: Sandy Louise Harling
In Residence: 1992

May I Take Your Order, Please? Good'ole southern gal Sandy was the actress/Shooters waitress who locked lips with Jake and then left town for the Big Apple when she landed on the fictional soap *Forever and Tomorrow* as Dr. Aviva Lester, halfway into the first *Melrose* season.

Post-Melrose: Can be seen in feature films like *Airheads* and *Acts of Love*. *Blue Sky*, with Jessica Lange and Tommy Lee Jones, was shot pre-*Melrose* (in 1991), but released after Locane left the show.

ANITA MORRIS

Red Hot Momma: Stella Hanson
In Residence: 1992

Sonny Boy: Mom showed up at Jake's birthday bash, to his chagrin. They kissed and made up before she croaked a season later, leaving half-brother Jess as Jake's messy inheritance.

VANESSA WILLIAMS

Who's That Girl? Rhonda Blair
In Residence: 1992–1993

Feel the Burn: Perky aerobics instructor Rhonda was a good idea that never took off. When not cast as the voice of social conscience, she was on a manhunt for Mr. Right. Rhonda eventually found rich hubby Terrence and they headed off to the 'burbs.

Appearing Weekly: As Lila, a legal receptionist and law student, on ABC's virtual reality drama *Murder One.* Here's a piece of trivia—this Vanessa Williams is *not* the former Miss America and musical star.

DEBORAH ADAIR

Pinstripe Princess: Lucy Cabot
In Residence: 1992–1993

Take a Memo: Alison's strict but wise D&D boss taught her the ropes of the corporate obstacle course. Then she married a guy named Irving and left town.

CC: After (and during) her *Melrose* tenure, Adair played Kate Roberts on *Days of Our Lives.* And here's a fun fact: she's married to *Melrose* producer Chip Hayes.

RAE DAWN CHONG

Neat Freak: Carrie Fellows
In Residence: 1992–1993

Control Queen: Melrose's hospital cornered-answer to Felix Unger, Carrie organized and alphabetized herself right out of Rhonda's apartment. An unwitting Terrence later hired the hyper-helper to decorate the dream house he bought for Rhonda.

SYDNEY WALSH

Character Sketch: Kay Beacon
In Residence: 1992–1993

On Pins and Needles: Jane's no-nonsense boss gave her underling a first chance to create her own designs. When Jane's marriage to Michael hit the skids, Kay pushed her back into the dating pool.

ROB ESTES

Hunk Alert: Sam Towler
In Residence: 1992–1993

Snapshot: Old friend Sam helped Jane get over the shock of discovering Michael's affair with Kimberly. Like a gentleman, he declined to take advantage of his distraught gal pal—ironic, of course, because Estes is Bissett's real life spouse.

Appeared Weekly: Until 1995 as the dashing star of the syndicated action series *Silk Stalkings*.

JAMES HANDY AND CLAUDETTE NEVINS

Pa and Ma: Matt Sr. and Constance Fielding
In Residence: 1992–1995

Out of the Closet: The 'rents had to adjust to the news of their son's sexual orientation, but they came around. Matt was grateful to bond with his father before Dad keeled over from congestive heart disease.

BEATA POZNIAK

Who's That Girlchik?   Dr. Katya Petrova
In Residence: 1993

To Emergency, STAT: To stay in the States, Dr. Katya trotted down the aisle with Matt Fielding. It put a crimp in his dating life, but he was gaga over her daughter Nikki (Mara Wilson). A family illness lured mother and child back to Russia.

Appearing Now: Polish Pozniak stars on the action-adventure CD-ROM game *The Psychic Detective* and runs an experimental theater group, Discordia Productions.

STEVEN ECKHOLDT

Hunk Alert: Robert Wilson
In Residence: 1993

May I Approach the Bench? Divorce lawyer-lover for Jane Mancini, Robert blundered into Michael's trap and got caught on tape making whoopee with one of Sydney's hooker pals.

Catch Him If You Can: Eckholdt joined *L.A. Law* for its swan song and appeared on the short-lived 1995 drama *The Monroes* as son James.

PARKER STEVENSON

Techno-Tool: Steve McMillan
In Residence: 1993

Get Your Modem Running: Computer king Steverino failed to win fair Alison away from her lovable lug Billy. He reformatted his er, diskette, and flew to Paris to expand his cyberspace.

Roll 'Em: Stevenson can be found behind the camera directing various television shows, including *Melrose*, and at home with wife Kirstie Alley and kids.

WILLIAM R. MOSES

The Shadow: Keith Gray
In Residence: 1993

Fatal Attraction: Sicko Keith stalked Alison, and finally blew his brains out. But is he really dead? We hope so.

Family Affair: Moses was married to Tracy Nelson, who played Alison's older sis, Meredith.

CASSIDY RAE

Pinup Girl: Sarah Owens
In Residence: 1993

Click! This younger poser brought Amanda back in contact with her estranged mother Hillary Michaels. Then the little bad luck charm's abusive beau, Hank, shoved a pregnant Jo down the stairs. Rae later joined Linda Gray on the short-lived *Models, Inc.*

MELANIE SMITH

She's Smokin':   Celia Morales
In Residence: 1993

Final Edit: Celia, a ciggie-smoking colleague of Billy's at *Escapade* magazine, bunked in with him and Alison while her condo was fumigated. Once the smoke cleared, Billy bested her for a promotion to New York City.

Out to Lunch

Who's fish and who's fowl? We've compiled a menu of who likes to eat what around the pool.

Billy: McDonald's
    Happy Meal
Brooke: Lobster & Paté
Alison: Anything in Wine
    Sauce
Jake: Swanson Hungry
    Man Dinners
Michael: Oysters
Sydney: Jelly Beans, Gum,
    Licorice, Popcorn
Matt: Kielbasa, Chestnuts
Amanda: Chinese Chicken
    Salad
Kimberly: Five-alarm Chili and
    a Banana Split
Jane: Ahi Tuna and a
    Goat Cheese Salad
Jo: Granola Bar and
    Snapple Iced Tea

Cammy Blackstone, DJ on KFRC-FM & AM in San Francisco:

As an addicted *Melrose* fanatic and radio announcer, I was very excited to see Kimberly's sudden career change from whiny mental patient to confident radio talk show host. While many radio jobs are scored by people being in the right place at the right time, getting a major market hosting job from a series of frantic psycho calls to Dr. Joyce Brothers' radio show is something that would only happen in the wacky world of *Melrose*.

Kimberly sure enjoyed her radio career while it lasted. The way she fondled the microphone and practically deep-throated it; the way her voice dropped seven octaves to Barry White depths when she opened the mike; her post-show meetings with her producer . . . my, my she sure got into her job. I have yet to find such a satisfying position in radio.

I did have a couple of problems with the radio station. Like, why did Kimberly answer her own phones? Even the most podunk 20-watt stations screen their calls before going on the air, or at least have a seven-second delay button. That sex-hungry producer should have been pre-screening Kimberly's calls to prevent wackos like Vic from getting on the air repeatedly.

And why was Vic the only caller? Are we supposed to believe that in the gigantic sprawling insanity of the L.A. metropolitan area, only one lone crazy guy would be listening and/or calling a talk show? Also, did the station just shut down after Kimberly's show? In real life, the next announcer would have walked in on Kimberly's savage trysting session. The whole thing was totally unrealistic, but then if it wasn't, it wouldn't be *Melrose Place*. By the way, my program director wants Kimberly to know that we do have a weekend shift open . . .

JOHN APREA

Hotel Magnate: Steve Bryant
In Residence: 1993

Check-In Time: Super-rich innkeeper Steve hosted Billy at his luxury resort for an *Escapade* interview, to the delight of his daughter Arielle (Terri Ivens). He let Billy and unexpected companion Alison enjoy the ritzy digs for the weekend.

KRISTIAN ALFONSO

Call Me Madam: Lauren Etheridge
In Residence: 1993–1994

Back at the Bordello: Taught Sydney what every good hooker should know. Quick learner Syd ran the show while Lauren pouted in the pokey. Once sprung, Lauren squashed her upstart pupil like a bug.

"Like Sands Through the Hourglass": Alfonso's back on *Days of Our Lives* as Hope Brady, the role she originated in 1983.

JAMES WILDER

Ahoy, Matey!   Reed Carter
In Residence: 1993–1994

Shipboard Shenanigans: Jo landed in a heap o' trouble when she hopped aboard Reed's boat, *The Pretty Lady*, a.k.a. Drug Central. Reed eventually slept with the fishes, but lived on as daddy to Jo's baby.

MEG WITTNER

Managing Editrix: Nancy Donner
In Residence: 1993–1994

Layout!: Wily *Escapade* boss Nancy put the moves on Billy, then fired him when he supplied Amanda with insider info to land the magazine's advertising account.

WAYNE TIPPIT

Car Czar: Palmer Woodward
In Residence: 1993–1994

Buckle Up: Amanda's no-good pop hired Jake to run his shady car restoration business. With the F.B.I. hot on his trail, Palmer plotted revenge against Hanson, but swallowed a bullet and died at sea instead.

THOM BIERDZ

Hunk: Hank
In Residence: 1993–1994

Shoving Match: Midwestern creep Hank came to L.A. and didn't like it, as girlfriend Sarah's friend Jo found out. He quickly skedaddled back to the prairie.

MONTE MARKHAM

Bad Dad: John Parker
In Residence: 1993–1994

Hands-on Parenting: Looking for love in all the wrong places, the Parker patriarch molested both of his daughters. Alison exposed the family's dirty little secret at a backyard barbecue.

TRACY NELSON

Sob Sister: Meredith Parker
In Residence: 1994

Home Movies: Big sister Meredith trekked back to Wisconsin with Alison to finger Daddy-O for molestation. Popping up in L.A. for a librarian's convention months later, the sight of studly Billy pulled her head out of the books, but he put her back on the shelf. Nelson is the daughter of pop star Rick Nelson, the son of TV's *Ozzie & Harriet* Nelson.

ERICH ANDERSON

The Good Doctor: Tom Miller
In Residence: 1994

Healing Hands: Alison's shrink seemed to have more than psychic relief on his mind when she consulted him about her recurring nightmares.

Remember When: Anderson played cartoonist Billy, who married Ellen during the last season of *thirtysomething*.

KATHY IRELAND

Water Babe: Brittany Maddocks
In Residence: 1994

Splish-Splash: Rising like Venus on the half shell, Ireland floated through four episodes in skimpy bikinis—befitting a *Sports Illustrated* model. She duped Jake, blew away Palmer Woodward and zoomed off into the night.

LINDA GRAY

Model Mom: Hillary Michaels
In Residence: 1994

Deep Freeze: High-powered model agency owner Hillary could not thaw out daughter Amanda, even when bailing her out of a nasty sex discrimination suit. Gray spun off into *Models, Inc.* but it tanked within one season.

JEFF KAAKE

Slimebucket: Chas Russell
In Residence: 1994

Just a Gigolo: Hillary's scummy boy toy put the moves on Amanda and then unsuccessfully sued D&D for sexual harassment after Amanda booted him out the firm.

CHERYL POLLACK

The Happy Homewrecker: Susan Madsen
In Residence: 1994

Cooking Up Trouble: Billy pissed off Alison when his hormones boiled over for her old friend, chef Susan. The girls came to blows with a nasty food fight during a D&D party catered by Susan. Meeow!

JASON BEGHE

On the Town: Jeffrey Lindley
In Residence: 1994

Aye, Aye, Popeye: Navy lieutenant Jeffrey leaned on Matt for strength when he came out to his commanding officer and parents. Later,

Locklear and Lovin' It

....

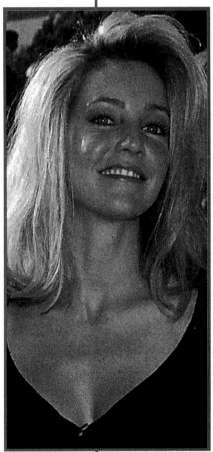

Week in and week out, Heather Dean Locklear, America's most popular exposed-roots blonde, works viewers into a phenom of a frenzy with her portrayal of ambitious, man-eating Amanda Woodward. Yet in real life, this messy-tressed, size-three beauty is one of the few genuinely *nice* people in Hollywood. It's practically impossible to find a colleague in front of or behind the camera with a bad word to say about her. Well, maybe Jack Wagner, who's less than thrilled with her penchant for garlic (see Wagner profile on page 121 for more scoop). More common is the attitude of *N.Y.P.D. Blue*'s Dennis Franz, her costar in the 1995 ABC true-crime movie *Texas Justice*, who told *Entertainment Weekly*, "There's just not a mean bone in that pretty little body of hers."

Locklear claims that the full-blown "Heather phenomenon" burst into full flower only recently. "I wasn't *Heather Locklear* until I got on this show," she told *Entertainment Weekly*. Originally, Locklear was tapped for only four episodes. It was 1992, and she was happy for the work. Interesting parts had become harder to nab since the eighties, when her shag could be spotted all over the tube.

Like many actors, Locklear at first paid the bills by appearing in numerous commercials for Sea and Ski, Coca-Cola, Pepsi, Polaroid (winking at James Garner), Tame creme rinse, and many others.

Wild child Heather Locklear has met her match in Bon Jovi's Richie Sambora.

After a string of guest shots on such now-classic seventies Spelling hits as *Hotel*, *The Love Boat*, and *Fantasy Island*, Locklear got her break in the purring package of Sammy Jo Carrington on *Dynasty* in 1981.

As Linda Evans's niece and Rock Hudson's daughter, Locklear grabbed audiences around the throat with her portrayal of Sammy Jo, the vixen from the wrong side of the tracks. She blithely sank her claws into Carrington heir-to-the-throne Steven—whose homosexual longings fell by the wayside in her lusty presence. Toying with Steven's heart, gleefully spending the Carrington millions, even casually abandoning her young son Danny (played by Matthew Lawrence, brother of *Blossom* heartthrob Joey), Locklear quickly learned that she could make nasty sexiness appealing (the snug wardrobe didn't hurt, either).

Even on *T.J. Hooker*, where she played earnest young cop Stacy Sheridan simultaneously with her Sammy Jo stint for four years, the producers couldn't resist showing off Locklear's mind-boggling physical attractions in skintight police uniforms unlike any seen on most cops. Amanda's shrink-wrapped clothes carry on this tradition—all her D&D business duds are specially shortened and form-fitted. Asked by *Entertainment Weekly* if Amanda's skirts are ever *too* short, Locklear breezily replied, "Probably not, as long as she doesn't have to sit down or bend over."

No one is more surprised by the success of this steamy, scheming persona than Locklear herself. She was raised in Los Angeles, a skinny kid with braces who didn't make it onto the Newbury Park High School cheerleading squad. She candidly admits to an almost overwhelming shyness that plagued her during her San Fernando Valley childhood. But what she may have lacked in self-confidence was made up for by the warmth and support of her family—father Bill, an administrator at U.C.L.A., mother Diane, who works at the Disney Studios, and older sibs Laurie, Colleen, and Mark.

Unlike Amanda's "motherless" childhood, Locklear enjoys her close-knit family. During her undergraduate days at U.C.L.A., she visited her dad daily and, even now, she frequently drops by her parents' house, only fifteen minutes from her own L.A. home. Mom and Dad often accompany her on publicity appearances as well. Locklear's also known for generously sharing her rustic Lake Arrowhead getaway (which was her family's vacation destination for years) with family and friends. But don't look for her to spend hours and hours poring over fabric swatches. When it came time to decorate, Locklear fearlessly marched into an L.A. store and furnished the whole joint on the spot—including a deer antler chandelier.

Life as Amanda Woodward, on the contrary, could not be more different. As she sashays from boardroom to bedroom, juggling men and business with equal parts ease and cynicism, Locklear has helped catapult the show into a hit. And the actress clearly revels in the out-of-this-world storylines that are the *Melrose* hallmark. "The whole show is evil! Everyone in it is evil: Matt's accused of murder; Kimberly is a nut. But the writers always have Amanda come out on top. I do love that," she admitted to *Entertainment Weekly*.

Fame does have its price, however. Anonymity is a thing of the past, even in jaded Los Angeles. Not only do the paparazzi like to snap Heather whenever possible (they snagged her last year at the airport—she was clutching a bag from N.Y.'s ultra-chic Henri Bendel department store), but stranger encounters befall her as well, as Heather related to *Entertainment Weekly*: "I was walking through the mall the other day. Now, if I think back a few years ago, even a year ago, I could walk anywhere. No problem. But this is a hit show, and people really are into the characters. I was going from one store to another. I had a hat on, tennis shoes, and workout clothes—hardly noticeable. But I could honestly see people stopping and looking and whispering. And you don't want to acknowledge it, 'cause you feel stupid, and I started getting into this panic. So I started walking faster and faster and then people were, like, chasing me, and I was so embarrassed. But I'm thinking, 'Oh, Heather, this is so stupid. What are they going to do, kill me?'"

Hardly. Fans only want to grab some of Heather's niceness (and Amanda's bitchiness) for themselves.

In the Bag

J ust what are the women of *Melrose* lugging around in their pocketbooks? Let's take a look.

In **Amanda**'s Prada tote:
- a microcassette dictation recorder
- cel phone
- teasing comb
- business card for her tailor (for those rush hem jobs)
- extra pantyhose
- D&D personnel list (for instant firings)
- Armani sunglasses

In **Alison**'s Gucci knockoff shoulder bag:
- airline-sized bottle of vodka
- twelve-step meeting calendar
- Visine and aspirin
- filofax
- diskette with résumé

In **Brooke**'s Escada (she's just gotta) clutch:
- picture of Daddy
- Tiffany key ring
- charge cards (in Daddy's name)— Neiman Marcus, Barney's, Bergdorf Goodman, AmEx Platinum card
- telephone number for limo service
- suicide hotline number

In **Jane**'s art portfolio:
- sketches
- fabric swatches
- engagement ring box
- Tic-tacs

In **Sydney**'s crocheted shoulder bag:
- bus schedule
- rollerskate key
- loose change
- bail bondsman's phone number
- nail file
- pack of matches
- Ray•Bans
- mini hairspray

In **Kimberly**'s black doctor bag:
- wiglet
- syringes
- bomb fuses
- set of universal car keys
- pager
- handcuffs

In **Jo**'s camera bag:
- picture of son Austin
- extra rolls of film
- can of mace
- DKNY sunglasses

resigned from the military, he and Matt shared a brief reunion when he confided his HIV-positive status.

CARMEN ARGENZIANO

Head Doctor: Stanley Levin
In Residence: 1994

He's an Old Cowhand: Dr. Mancini thought he had Levin by the er . . . you know, when Levin's name turned up in Madam Lauren's little black book. Mancini tracked down Levin's favorite date, who confessed to playing a different version of Cowboys and Indians with him on a regular basis. To make sure that he'd get the chief residency appointment, Mancini showed up with Levin's cowgirl call girl for the big announcement. One look at his little cowpoke and Levin handed the chief residency reins over to a happy Michael.

CHRISTOPHER GARTIN

I'll Be Your Handyman: Ted Ryan
In Residence: 1994

Peeping Tom: Ted slithered around the building as Amanda's sneaky handyman. He put his tools to kinky use, drilling holes to spy on the *Melrose* lovelies. Jo and Amanda trapped him and exacted an *Extremities*-like revenge, tying him up and threatening to gouge his eyes out.

TY MILLER

Buss Boy: Rob
In Residence: 1994

Matt's Best Man: Rob flew to L.A. for college roommate Billy's wedding to Alison. Matt squired Rob around town and the two shared the infamous slo-mo kiss, witnessed by a stunned Billy.

ANDREW WILLIAMS

Dude From Down Under: Chris Marchette
In Residence   1994–1995

To Catch A Thief: More bad luck for Jane. While chastely wooing her, Aussie businessboy Chris drained Mancini Designs of its assets, kidnapped Sydney, and forced her to be his Las Vegas playmate.

STANLEY KAMEL

Whip-Cracker: Bruce Teller
In Residence: 1994–1995

Final Curtain: Chief Bruce got the last laugh in the ultimate D&D battle with Amanda when he hanged himself in her office. She cut him down and plopped into the prez's recliner, pronto.

Check Your Local Listings: Kamel's pulled double duty on Fox's *Beverly Hills 90210* as hooligan Tony Marchette and on ABC's *Murder One* as the shrink among the sharks.

BRIAN BLOOM

Spin Doctor: Zach Philips
In Residence: 1994–1995

One Hit Wonder: Another of Alison's sorry suitors. Party maniac Zach, a music industry exec, sweet-talked her into assorted drunken sprees. Two aspirin and cup o' joe, please.

DAVID JAMES ELLIOTT

Quarterback Cutie: Terry Parsons
In Residence: 1994–1995

Block That Pass: Terry was a recovering alcoholic and sex-addicted football star whom Alison met in rehab. He proposed, but all they had in common was their former love affairs with bottles of booze.

Saturday Night Fever: Elliott's now starring on NBC's *J.A.G.* weekly and met up with Daphne Zuniga on the 1995 NBC movie *Degree of Guilt.*

TOM SCHANLEY

Good Cop/Bad Cop: Jonathan Rawlings
In Residence: 1994–1995

On the Beat: Sympathetic cop Jonathan helped Matt after a gay bashing incident. Jo saw his darker side when she rode shotgun in his squad car and snapped pix of him viciously beating a drug suspect. Panicked, he held Jo and Matt hostage until gun-girl Jo grabbed his weapon and Matt called the cops.

JANET CARROLL

Midwest Mom: Marion Shaw
In Residence: 1994–1995

She's Got a Secret: In season two, Marion fooled Michael into believing her daughter Kimberly had died in Ohio following their car crash. By season four, Peter had Marion spilling her guts to solve the riddle of Kimberly's psychosis. She spoke her piece and fled back home.

PENNY FULLER AND JERRY HARDIN

Family Fued: Marilyn and Dennis Carter
In Residence: 1994–1995

Playing for Keeps: Goodwill wore thin when Reed's parents sued Jo for custody of her unborn child. After a bitter struggle, Jo put her son up for adoption.

ANTOINETTE BYRON

Nifty Nanny: Emily Baldwin
In Residence: 1995

Baby Mine: Jo's Mary Poppins was secretly on the payroll for Reed's twisted parents. She kidnapped the baby and took him to his grandparents, but Jo tracked them down.

JASMINE GUY

Make It Snappy: Caitlin Mills
In Residence: 1995

Cut-the Coffee Break: Efficiency expert Caitlin blew through *Melrose* in several budget-slashing episodes. She toppled Amanda off her cushy perch at D&D, but was exposed as Peter Burns's partner in deceit and skulked out of town.

ZITTO KAZANN

Psycho Pal: Henry
In Residence: 1995

A Figment of Her Imagination?: Kazann played "Henry," Kimberly's gardener-turned-rapist-turned-psychotic alter ego. We hope he's gone for good.

DAN CORTESE

Bad Seed Brother: Jess Hanson
In Residence: 1995

Sibling Rivalry: Black sheep Jess's romance with Jo turned violent and Jake went after him. The pair did a two-step off the edge of a high-rise beam and Jess didn't live to finish the dance.

DAVID BEECROFT

Doublecrossing Doc: Paul Graham
In Residence: 1995

Frameup: Matt thought it was love, but it was a setup when this scummy plastic surgeon fingered him for the murder of wife Carolyn. He 'fessed up as he took his last breath.

DANA SPARKS

Devoted Wife: Carolyn Graham
In Residence: 1995

Unsuspecting Spouse: Paul's trusting wife ended up bludgeoned to death by an antique candlestick. As he lay dying, Paul admitted it was his handiwork that did her in.

TRACI LORDS

Cult Cutie: Rikki
In Residence: 1995

True Believer: Sydney got in over her head with roomie Rikki's cult. And she was messy, too—just ask Jake about the time she left Shooters in shambles.

On the Silver Screen: Don't blink, or you'll miss the ex-porn star in *Virtuosity.*

RAMY ZADA

Ungodly Guru: Martin Abbot
In Residence: 1995

Master Zealot: The guru at Rikki's cult camp, Martin did fun things like burying Sydney in a locked box until she submitted to his wishes.

Andrew Shue and Grant Show pal around at the Clinton/Gore campaign caravan in 1992.

Jane and Jake came to her rescue, and Syd shot out the tires to keep the loonies from recapturing her.

DR. JOYCE BROTHERS

The Kooky Doc: Plays herself
In Residence: 1995

Shrink Rapped: The ubiquitous psychologist appeared periodically as herself, with Kimberly as a caller to her radio therapy show.

MACKENZIE PHILLIPS

Boot Camp Babe: Maureen Dodd
In Residence: 1995

Soldier Girl: Maureen crossed swords with Kimberly at "No More Victims," the feminist paramilitary training course. She was thrilled when Kimberly took a hike back to L.A.

MORGAN BRITTANY

Designing Woman: Mackenzie Hart
In Residence: 1995

Bombs Away: Richard Hart's Donna Karan-like wife tracked him down at Jane's apartment just as Kimberly's explosion hit. She suffered a fatal heart attack at the scene—much to Jane's barely suppressed delight.

HUDSON LEICK

Siren Sister-in-Law: Shelly Hanson
In Residence: 1995

Hankerin' Hussy: Jess's ex-wife showed up unexpectedly on Jake's doorstep and did her seductive best to peel him off Jo while she embezzled his business funds.

FRANCIS X. MCCARTHY

Chief Bigot: Dr. Hobbs
In Residence: 1995

He's Outta There: After Matt's homosexuality was revealed following the murder frameup, homophobe Hobbs fired him. At a preliminary deposition Matt's lawyer goaded Hobbs into repeating his slur in front of witnesses—and soon he was medical history.

ANTONIO SABATO JR.

Big Italian Lug: Jack Parezi
In Residence: 1995

Miami Vice: Amanda's abandoned gangster husband found his long-lost beloved, thanks to Brooke's snooping. The wife-abuser made noises about a divorce, but just couldn't get Amanda off his mind 'til death did them part.

PERRY KING

Daddy Dearest: Hayley Armstrong
In Residence: 1995
Captain of Industry: Hayley's marriage to Alison made his little girl Brooke pea-green with envy, but Brooke took solace in Dad's divorcing Alison right before his untimely death.

JOHN ENOS III

Good Fella: Bobby Parezi
In Residence: 1995–96

Make Me An Offer: Jack's brother Bobby was Amanda's first love. After Jack's death, Bobby was supposed to kill her on behalf of "the family" to avenge Jack, but ended up winning her back instead.

COMING ATTRACTIONS:

Priscilla Presley, Loni Anderson, Hunter Tylo and more . . .

Overleaf: Left, a blithesome Josie Bissett with much-beloved hubby Rob Estes. Right, Thomas Calabro: "I like all the girls on *Melrose Place*, but I'm not remotely attracted to any of them." (at Aaron Spelling's Christmas party with wife Elisabeth.)

True Romance

Characters on the show might bed hop with abandon, but away from the set, the stars of *Melrose* have found long-lasting romance to be far more satisfying.

HEATHER LOCKLEAR

Main Squeeze: Husband Richie Sambora of Bon Jovi. On December 17, 1994, Heather and Richie were wed at the American Cathedral in Paris (following a small ceremony two days earlier at Richie's Rumson, New Jersey, home). Heather glided down the aisle in a satin and lace halter dress with bolero jacket, courtesy of *Dynasty* costumer Nolan Miller. Wedding guests enjoyed two lavish parties—on the eve of the Big Day at the St. James Club with Remy Martin Louis XIII Cognac flowing and a post-ceremony champagne fete at the Paris Ritz.

He's History: Ex-husband Tommy Lee of Motley Crüe. Do we detect a pattern here? Tommyboy is now husband to Pamela Anderson, überbabe of *Baywatch*.

In her dating days, Heather was linked to Tom Cruise, Scott Baio, Mark Harmon, and Andrew Stevens.

Words of Love: "I've got the best man in the world at home right now waiting for me." (*Entertainment Weekly*)

ANDREW SHUE

Main Squeeze: His wife, Jennifer Hageney.

Jennifer and Andrew met in the fall of 1994: she was his agent at the high-powered United Talent Agency. Now someone else is managing Shue at UTA, and Jennifer, three years Shue's senior, has the enviable task of managing her hubby's personal life. They married on October 7, 1995, in Swan Lake, Montana, on a strip of land owned by Shue. The dress was formal—Shue sported a tux, Hageney an off-the-shoulder, full-length gown. Word has it that they've been keeping busy—Jennifer's now expecting!

She's History: Courtney Thorne-Smith. The castmates shared a romance off the set during the show's first season. They have nothing but kind words for one another since shifting to friendship. "Courtney was amazingly supportive during one of the most chaotic, changing years of my life," Shue told *TV Guide.*

COURTNEY THORNE-SMITH

Current Squeeze: Actor and fellow golf buff Drew Pillsbury.

He's History: Andrew Shue. "We were two nice kids under this incredible stress. I don't know if I could have gotten through it without him. We had a light, fun, sweet relationship. We'll always have a close bond. [But] when one of us gets married, that'll be hard," Thorne-Smith told *People.*

GRANT SHOW

Current Squeeze: Laura Leighton

She's History: Yasmine Bleeth, the raven haired *Baywatch* beauty, who's engaged to actor and singer Ricky Paull Goldin.

Behind Closed Doors: Grant and Laura share a home together. "It's funny to read stories that are people's ideas of who we are, because these stories reflect an imaginary Sydney-and-Jake relationship. It's just been made-up goofy stuff," Leighton told *Entertainment Weekly.*

> "*Melrose Place* is another great, big wonderful mobile suspending all the beautiful characters in space, where that wizard of intrigue, Aaron Spelling, moves them about, blowing his tornadic plot breezes, keeping everyone and everything in constant motion."—Phyllis Diller, comedienne

JOSIE BISSETT

Main Squeeze: Hubby Rob Estes, late of *Silk Stalkings.*

First Impressions: Seeing Rob at a movie audition in January 1991, Bissett was immediately smitten. "I was just goo-goo over him. I can still remember him coming out of the elevator and exactly what he was wearing," she bubbled to *TV Guide*. It was a scant two months before Bissett and Estes set up housekeeping. By Thanksgiving, he'd popped the question in the snow at Big Bear, a California mountain resort. The couple tied the knot in Bissett's hometown, Seattle, among 170 guests on May 1, 1992.

Our Happy Home: Josie and Rob enjoy life away from the soundstage at a two-level, deluxe Santa Monica condo.

Paging Donna Reed: Plans to feather the nest with the patter of little feet are definitely in the works. Once her *Melrose* contract is up, Josie wants to get cracking on starting a family with Rob. "I want a boy and a girl. I want to finish [the fourth] season, do a miniseries, and then get pregnant during my last season on *Melrose* so I can have the baby when it's over," she outlined to *TV Guide*. Good luck, and let the Games begin!

DAPHNE ZUNIGA

Current Squeeze: Billy Marti, an actor and chef

Mad About the Boy: They met through mutual friends, and the romance is going strong. "He's a wonderful cook, a giving man, and he makes me laugh. I don't know why I took so long to find him," Daphne gushed to *People*.

MARCIA CROSS

Someone to Watch Over Me: Marcia made millions of women all over America nod in understanding when she told *Entertainment Weekly*, "You think that just because I'm in Hollywood and have a show I should have the perfect guy? Not true. It doesn't work that way. I haven't met the right person yet."

JACK WAGNER

Main Squeeze: Wife Kristina Malandro

Meeting Cute: The place: the set of *General Hospital*; the time: 1984. Frisco was a singer, Felicia the young ingenue searching for Aztec treasure. The chemistry between Jack Wagner and Kristina Malandro was palpable to everyone, including the actors themselves.

The courtship was whirlwind, culminating in the birth of their first son, Petey, in 1990. They eloped to Lake Tahoe on December 18, 1993—

with Kristina wearing a dress borrowed from the *GH* wardrobe department. The couple spent their wedding night in Las Vegas. Their second son, Harrison, arrived in December of 1994.

THOMAS CALABRO

Main Squeeze: Wife Elisabeth Pryor, a writer

Taking Chances: As soon as Calabro set eyes on Pryor, he knew she was the cream in his coffee. Pryor wasn't so sure, however, and tried to give him the heave-ho. But Calabro was persistent: he cajoled his agent into wrangling her phone number. He then called, pretending to be a producer so she'd call him back. It worked. They married in 1994.

"I like all the girls [on *Melrose Place*]," Calabro told *TV Guide*. "But I'm not remotely attracted to any of them. My wife is the woman of my life."

And Baby Makes Three: Daughter Conner Shea was born in 1995.

Who's that girl? An ultra-protective Doug Savant won't let anyone know his wife's name.

Peter has just posted Michael's bail.

PETER: It must feel great to be at home.

MICHAEL: Yeah. I just wish I didn't still have a noose hangin' around my neck. I hate women. Correction—I hate all the women I've even been in love with.

———————

Then Peter drops a little bombshell on Michael.

PETER: Oh, by the way, seeing as we're getting along so well, I thought that as a courtesy I'd let you know that I'm dating your ex-wife. I'll refer to her by name to avoid any confusion—Kimberly.

MICHAEL: Are you crazy? Because she is.

———————

Knowing Amanda wants to can her from D&D, a drunk Alison bursts in on Billy and Susan's romantic dinner.

ALISON: What's the occasion? Screw-Alison-out-of-a-fiancé Day? Screw-Alison-out-of-a-promotion Day? Or, let's just dump on Alison for the heck of it?

———————

Michael stops in at Mancini Designs to talk Sydney into divorce.

SYDNEY: Looks like the sleazebag hall of fame is missing a member. Now what would bring vermin like you out into the daylight? I know—you want to apologize.

MICHAEL: No, Syd. I want a divorce.

SYDNEY: And I want to wake up tomorrow morning and sing like Aretha Franklin. Do the words "go to hell" mean anything to you?

———————

Alison asks Billy what he sees in Elisabeth, the eager office intern.

BILLY: She's you, two years ago.

———————

Michael gives Sydney a check for $5,000 and gets her to sign divorce papers.

MICHAEL: Here's your five grand. Taking money for *not* having sex—new low, don't you think?

———————

Jake accuses Jo of being a pill with her complaint that he pay more attention to her.

JAKE: I have really had it with all the petty garbage around here. All of you just keep rehashing it. You sling it from one apartment to the next. You know, the self-absorption is a bottomless pit in this place.

———————

Michael tries to talk Jane out her romance with Chris.

MICHAEL: I know how you are when you're getting it regular. Nothing else matters.

JANE: You disgust me. Get out.

———————

Jo tells Amanda she has won the contest over Jake.

JO: And you know what, Amanda? I've had it with this tug of war over Jake. I'm throwing in the towel. So you can have him. Forever, if you'd like. From now on Mr. Washboard is yours.

———————

Amanda kids Alison about bolting from her wedding.

AMANDA: Alison, don't I recall something about you being on a honeymoon? Oh, that's right, you have to be married to have a honeymoon. So, have your feet warmed up yet, or are they still cold? You certainly do lead an exciting life. I do; I don't; I do again.

———————

Amanda's shocked when she meets Brittany Maddocks aboard Jake's boat.

AMANDA: Permission to come aboard, Captain Jake.
BRITTANY: Can I give him a message?
AMANDA: Yeah. Tell him he's a lying pig.

And Jake lets Brittany know it caused all kinds of trouble.

JAKE: Yeah, well, I just walked into a buzzsaw at the apartment, thanks to you.

But Brittany persists, and wins the battle to wear Jake down.

BRITTANY: You've been with possessive, jealous, clinging women. Women who want something from you. . . . What you've needed all along was a woman who only wanted to give you pleasure, who only wanted to do what you wanted to do, who only wanted to make you happier than you've ever been in your life.

Jo's disgusted by Jake's young date at a poolside party.

JO: What do you call a woman like that? She's too young to be a tramp. A bimbo?
JANE: How about whore?

Jo and Jake move in together, but Jo's sure the sizzle has left the relationship as they sit silently at the dinner table.

JO: This is my fear. This, sitting here and having absolutely nothing, nothing to say to each other. I mean, we've lived together for—what?—two days and already we're out of material.
JAKE: My mouth was full.

Joel, the art gallery owner, backs off from continuing to date Matt because he's married.

JOEL: I just worry that, you know, your life is a little too complicated for me. I mean, it's tough enough being gay without having a wife and a kid to worry about.

Daphne Zuniga: "Maybe *Melrose Place* is the thinking person's nighttime soap."

Alison is running door to door trying to find out where her abruptly departed roommate is in the very first episode. She knocks on Jake's door.

JAKE: Why is it that every time a girl doesn't show up at night people think she's in my apartment?

———————

Potential new roommate Billy explains why he needs to move away from home.

BILLY: I mean, I'm starting to feel like this sexually repressed, totally frustrated newt.

———————

Billy and Alison try to get the ground rules straight when he first moves into the apartment.

BILLY: But now what happens when I bring a babe home and, you know, bada-bing, bada-bang, and we're going at it here on this couch?

———————

Rhonda and Matt talk before she goes on a date. Matt reviews her outfit for the evening.

MATT: Ow. Hurt me. I want details.
RHONDA: Honey, I'm praying for details.

———————

Alison gets in a little over her head when her boss, Hal Barber, takes her to a D&D event for a client. He worms his way into her apartment afterward.

HAL: Alison, did I ever mention that aside from being smart and ambitious, I also find you extremely sexy?
ALISON: Oh, trust me, I'm not.

———————

Alison has a fit when Billy and Susan begin dating.

ALISON: I hope you're being careful with her, Billy.
BILLY: What do you mean?
ALISON: I wouldn't want you to catch anything. Back in college, the frat boys used to call her Round Heel Susie 'cause it only took a little nudge to get her on her back.
BILLY: You're drunk.
ALISON: Yeah, well, you're a self-centered pig. At least in the morning I'll be sober.

———————

And Alison lets Susan know what she thinks, too.

ALISON: You are about as good for him as your cooking—in other words, you stink.

Amanda escapes Michael's blackmail threats by telling Peter herself about the unsavory things she said about him on tape.

AMANDA: Do you hate me? For not being truthful with you?
PETER: On the contrary, I have a deep passion for liars.

Sydney cannot believe Michael wants to dump her for back-from-the-dead Kimberly.

SYDNEY: That's it? Zombie woman lives and you drop everything and go running back to her?

Poor blind Alison can't tell what great flowers Billy sent; Amanda interprets.

AMANDA: Oh my god, Alison, you're gonna wanna keep this arrangement. You should see it. It's bigger than a Buick.

Amanda asks Peter why he's helping Kimberly out so much.

PETER: I realize that people matter, too.
AMANDA: Oh, then you must be the new and improved Peter Burns.

Of course, matters get worse when Brooke discovers Billy helping Alison rebutton her blouse.

BROOKE: Oh, so now you're dressing her. What's next, sponge baths?

Jake asks Jo what happened after he got drunk at Shooters trying to ease his guilt about Jess's death.

JO: Oh, I'd say after much conversation, I tucked you in around two.
JAKE: You gotta be kidding me. I don't have that much to say about anything.

Michael's tricked Sydney again by seducing her so he can drive Kimberly crazy while she's under arrest.

MICHAEL: Sydney, get lost.

Doug Savant

Whenever a gay character is introduced on a prime-time television show, it's an instant attention-grabber for the actor playing the part—and at the start of *Melrose Place*, Doug Savant was no exception. As one of prime time's few openly homosexual characters, Matt Fielding *has* broken down barriers. But while the straight *Melrose* denizens romp with abandon, Matt has often been left behind— a politically correct character in search of sizzling story.

Doug Savant has the acting chops to change all that. He came to the show a seasoned performer. His television credits range from *Knots Landing* (where he appeared as a young Mack Mackenzie in flashbacks) to *China Beach* to *Cagney & Lacey*. On the big screen, he played pivotal roles in *Hanoi Hilton*, *Shaking the Tree*, *Paint It Black*, and *Red Surf*. As Officer Mike McGill in the thriller *Masquerade*, he netted third billing after Rob Lowe and Meg Tilly.

Flashy roles aside, before *Melrose* hit, Savant was punching the clock as a pizza deliveryman—so making the jump to being a prime-time regular has allowed him to use his car for pursuits other than dropping off pepperoni pies. A self-confessed knucklehead with little social awareness during his southern California adolescence, Savant played quarterback on his high school football team. He attended U.C.L.A. before dropping out to chase a full-time acting career.

Married and the father of two children (although years ago, he was fixed up with an adolescent Nancy McKeon from *The Facts of Life*), Savant likes to keep a low-profile. As he earnestly told *Rolling Stone*: "I've gone out of my way to keep my personal life private because of the nature of my character. There are other straight actors who have played gay characters and then shouted their straightness to the media at every chance. I think that's disgraceful. I have the responsibility to play the common humanity that crosses boundaries of sexuality."

Savant's lofty intentions for his character have not always panned out. During the first bumpy season, the writers seemed unsure with what to do with both Matt and Rhonda, the energetic aerobics instructor portrayed by Vanessa Williams, now on Steven Bochco's *Murder One*. The result was often a parade of scenes where Matt tagged along as Rhonda's personal cheerleader. When Williams was written off the show, it was nail-biting time for Savant. "I had *nothing* to do. I'd just go '*Yes*, Rhonda,' or '*Good*, Rhonda,' or '*Go get* 'em, Rhonda.' [Without her around] I was like 'Help me, Rhonda,'" Savant admitted to *Rolling Stone*.

After a series of quick, go-nowhere romances, Matt landed in boiling hot water as a murder defendant at the start of the fourth season. The devious twist that pinned him down was classic *Melrose* back-stabbing, and he was thrilled. "I'm excited about the opportunity for Matt to have some teeth," he crowed to *Entertainment Weekly*. "With Matt and other gay characters, we're back in the Lucy and Ricky days [of early television]. It will be an evolution. I'm just a bump on the highway."

Savant is obviously intent on expanding his career beyond the confines of the *Melrose* apartment complex. Last fall, he stretched his acting wings in a new direction, as a rapist/serial murderer in NBC's *Fight for Justice: The Nancy Conn Story*. "My greatest hope is that I'm unrecognizable," Savant told *People* about his latest foray. "I've been the moral conscience on *Melrose* for years, so I wanted to play a man without one."

SYDNEY: What? I don't understand.

MICHAEL: I only said and did what I had to to get you in the right mood for our little visit. You see, even catatonic, Kimberly could see through any charade. So that had to be real love in your eyes. But now that Kimberly's back in Babbleville, your usefulness has run out.

SYDNEY: Oh, God, I haven't learned anything, have I?

MICHAEL: Apparently not.

Jo confides her frustrations about Shelly to Jane.

JO: Last night could have been perfect. Jake was in the pool. I was about to go get changed to get in with him and then Shelly walks out of his apartment with this string bikini she spray-painted on—carrying a towel and a beer.

She later raises the topic with Jake.

JO: Excuse me? What is this double standard here? I mean, I saw Shelly in her butt floss bikini saunter on into your apartment for coffee yesterday. I felt a stab of jealousy, but I just kept it to myself.

Brooke weighs her options with Alison about her dating Hayley.

BROOKE: If you and Daddy are involved, then maybe it's time for us to bury the hatchet.

ALISON: Gee, you'd have to pull it out of my back first.

Jo and Jane go a few rounds about who's got the worse love life.

JANE: After Reed and Jess, you're the last person who should be giving anyone advice on relationships.

JO: I have made mistakes. That's why I'm trying to tell you.

JANE: Yeah, well, please don't. My worst fear is that my life could turn out like yours.

Billy defends his bride to Alison, who is not impressed.

ALISON: What? So now I'm part of some dark anti-Brooke conspiracy? Billy, even if I did want to join, she's made so many enemies there isn't any room left on the grassy knoll.

Brooke goes nuts when she realizes Hayley spent the night at Alison's.

    ALISON: If you're so interested in other people's sex lives, there's a 976 number you can call.

Unlike Brooke, Billy doesn't want to hear the gory details.

    ALISON: He's got a five-star chef at the mansion.
    BILLY: Well, maybe you can bring me a doggie bag sometime.

Shelly and Jo have a chat at the bar.

    SHELLY: Do you know anything about computers, Jo?
    JO: Just that they're good for playing games with. Don't strangle yourself on all those cords, Shelly.

A very drunk Amanda gives Peter a hard time when he tries to get out of her apartment.

    AMANDA: No, no, no, you have to put me to bed first. Please.
    PETER: Amanda, come on . . . no, no, this is not a good idea. Hold on . . . hey, hey, not a good idea.
    AMANDA: I want to be undressed for bed.
    PETER: Well, be my guest.
    AMANDA: No, be *mine*.

Jane's upset that Chris keeps putting her off.

    JANE: What is it? I don't understand. What's wrong with me? Why don't you ever want to make love to me? . . . Now cut out the sensitive crap and just take me.

Jake and Jo are on the outs—again—over Jane's new love, Richard Hart.

    JAKE: You're going to sleep with Richard. Or is it Dick now?

Looking for Love in All the Wrong Places

By the third season of *Melrose Place* the writers proved that they could—and would—concoct plots further out than Jupiter. No character was safe from a personality overhaul. No pair, no triangle, no quadrangle was unimaginable. If you blinked, you missed major storylines. So buckle up; it's a bumpy ride revisiting the mayhem and merriment.

REDHEADS IN TROUBLE

Michael came to with a raging case of amnesia after being hit by Jane's car. Kimberly stowed her broomstick in a corner and anxiously hovered, while also assuring her frantic sidekick Sydney that their alibi would be their long, cozy lunch at the Farmer's Market. Later, a horrified Sydney overheard Kimberly blithely reporting to the cops that she had spent the entire afternoon at the U.S.C. medical library. Sydney was arrested after the cops searched her apartment and found the blonde wig Kimberly had planted there.

Back at the beach house with Michael, Kimberly carefully edited her account of his life before the accident. Throwing herself into the role of beloved fiancée, she merrily assassinated the characters of everyone else in his life. Kimberly's devoted stance convinced the police they had fingered the right suspect.

Sydney could not catch a break to save her sorry life. When her daddy George came to town, he refused to post her bail. She lashed out at him with an angry accusation of neglect—as long as he had his perfect child Jane, he didn't care about her. If she really had wanted to kill someone, it should have been him, Syd ranted. Stung and appalled by her outburst, George and Jane arrived at the sad conclusion that Sydney would be best off at a psychiatric facility. After a short, but extremely loud, straightjacketed trip, she found herself locked up at the Hidden Hills Sanitarium.

Sydney's lawyer tried to convince Jane that her sister should plea bargain her way out of the sanitarium. Sydney refused, but a late-night visit

Laura Leighton: "Everybody has the potential to be bitchy, you know. The way I see it, Syd's not *bad*. She has her reasons."

from a horny ward attendant persuaded her that parole would be better than submitting to his minimum-wage advances. She confessed, agreed to abide by Jane's sniveling supervision, and was released.

As Kimberly and Michael stood in front of their favorite restaurant, a carful of teenagers swerved right at them. The scare tripped off an exact replay of Michael's accident. In a snap, he recognized the face of the driver who'd hit him as none other than his devoted fiancée. With his memory fully restored, Michael and Kimberly circled one another warily, until he finally taunted her with a choice—she could love him or kill him. Naturally, sex won out.

Eager to pursue his twisted lovematch with Kimbo, Michael demanded a divorce from Sydney. He offered to buy her out with a paltry five thou; she countered with a demand for his half-interest in Mancini Designs. Michael pretended to agree to Sydney's terms and arranged a meeting at a hotel to seal the deal. A surprised Sydney was greeted with ardent kisses and promises of holding together their marriage. She eagerly signed the papers, that foolish redhead. Nice going, babe, Michael told her snidely. You just signed away your rights to everything. Syd's love balloon had been punctured again.

After a quickie Vegas wedding, Kimberly and Michael returned to the hospital to face the ire of the new chief of staff, Dr. Peter Burns. Mikey was fired for leaving town while on call.

Furious, Michael devised a plot to get Amanda to lure Dr. Burns, one of her latest flirtations, into rehiring him—the payoff for her being his one-half interest in Mancini Designs. Amanda hotfooted over to Jane, who jumped at the chance to ditch Michael from the firm. But when Michael showed up at the Mancini offices to sign over his interest, he got the last laugh by playing a surreptitiously recorded tape of Amanda dissing both Peter and Jane. On the tape, Amanda was in full-on nasty mode, calling Jane a fool and Peter her plaything. Michael marched off with his interest in the business and future blackmail leverage over Amanda intact.

INCEST, A GAME THE WHOLE FAMILY CAN PLAY

Having fled her own wedding, Alison was holed up in San Francisco with her sister Meredith. As the twosome conspired to avenge their detested dad's wrongdoings, they were unaware that he was watching their comings and goings. When Meredith went out to pick up some Chinese (haven't they heard of free delivery? in *San Francisco*?), Pops made his move and slipped into the apartment. An unsuspecting Alison shrieked in terror as he lunged for her. His taunts came to an end when Meredith reappeared, gun in hand. Billy, after realizing that Alison had run off to her sister's, had gone to San Fran as well, and burst in as backup.

Billy brought Alison back to L.A., where she told her lovable lug that she appreciated his support, but was determined to resolve her childhood trauma on her own. Even Billy's valiantly romantic suggestion—that they spirit off to Vegas and get hitched—was turned down. She took off for Wisconsin with just Meredith in tow.

Meredith was skittish about their chances of defeating Dad on his own turf. John's small-town cronies wouldn't believe that their neighbor could have done such horrible things to his own little darlings. When the sisters arrived at the judge's chambers and saw their parents emerge from a backslapping session with the chuckling magistrate, even Alison had to admit that a legal victory looked chancy.

Before riding back to the airport, however, Alison dropped by her parent's house and laid a stink bomb in the middle of their jolly barbecue. Her public accusations toward her father broke him, and he turned on his wife, blaming her coldness for forcing him to turn to his children for unnatural affection. The horrified friends and neighbors shrank from the scene, and Alison felt vindicated at last.

WHAT MAKES AMANDA RUN?

Amanda, ambitious as salmon swimming upstream, found a soulmate in ruthless Dr. Peter Burns. He masterminded a strategy to take over D&D and install her as president. Her boss Bruce unwittingly helped get the ball rolling by suffering a heart attack in the middle of a business party full of clients. Seizing her moment, Amanda stepped in and kept the clients happy, all the while insisting to Bruce that she was shielding news of his bad health from them. In fact, she lost no time telling one and all about his weak heart, while promoting herself as his logical successor.

Outside the office, Peter was busily buying up D&D stock to position himself for a takeover. When his coup was accomplished, Amanda smugly ascended to the top. Bruce took the news badly—he hanged himself in his office. Getting his last digs in, he pinned a note to his sleeve: "Congratulations on your promotion."

Coldhearted Amanda brusquely turned away Bruce's sister, Donna, when she requested money to keep Bruce's children in college. Sorry—no pension, no money, no nothing, Amanda told her. As the winter hol-

Overleaf: The Usual Suspects.

idays approached, Amanda nursed a foul flu in bed, thrashing under the spell of a long feverish nightmare. A ghostly Bruce floated in the air, pointing out the sorrow she would reap if she continued on her greedy, self-centered path. The images were potent enough to cause a change of heart, and Amanda gave a grateful Donna the money she had asked for. Hell, she was even kind to Alison. Talk about Christmas spirit!

Amanda's free reign at D&D ground to a swift halt when she rebuffed Peter. In retaliation, he hired efficiency expert Caitlin Mills, who stormed the offices. None of Amanda's views match Caitlin's—especially her advice about firing alcoholic Alison. Seemed Caitlin, a card-carrying AA member, would keep Alison's perch secure.

Billy was Caitlin's clear favorite—she was ready to clear out most of the staff except for him. He unwittingly kept Amanda apprised of which heads were likely to roll. Anxious to hold onto her power, she shredded reports that reflected badly on her leadership. Peter gave Caitlin, his lover, the green light to ax Amanda, but in the end he couldn't resist doing it himself.

Caitlin ordered drug tests for the staff. Amanda's results showed marijuana in her bloodstream. She accused Peter of doctoring the antibiotics he had insisted she take. Fishing out a capsule that had rolled under her dresser, Amanda brought it to trusty Matt to have it analyzed at the hospital. A chagrined Peter was confronted with this damning evidence and the board dismissed the overzealous Caitlin in haste.

Time healed the rift between Amanda and Michael, so that when she needed some medical sleuthing to bury Peter further, Michael was her hospital gumshoe. He snooped around and discovered—gasp—that Peter was accepting kickbacks. Sniffing a payoff of his own, Michael reported to Amanda that nothing was amiss and then put the screws to Peter while they were out on the golf links. Within moments, Michael was heading up a bogus scientific project of his own.

Luba Reeves, owner of multiple-unit apartment buildings in San Francisco:

Q. Would you allow a woman who blew up one of your buildings to move into an apartment after you rebuilt the premises? And could you rebuild the complex in one month?

A. Are you kidding me? I'd slap a restraining order on that woman so she couldn't get within 100 feet of the building. The idea that she'd move into one of the apartments is totally sick. Hey, an apartment building is a major investment; you wouldn't let some crazy woman who blew it up *near* the place.

Rebuilding in one month is a total fantasy. It would take that long just to deal with City Hall for your permits.

Peter took revenge by sedating Amanda at the hospital and telling Michael she would never leave Burns's operating room alive. Michael intervened and Amanda survived.

But Peter and Michael weren't out of each other's well-moussed hair yet. Kimberly had trumped-up charges of attempted murder brought against Michael following her aborted suicide incident. Peter bailed Michael out of prison, to the tune of $200,000. All he asked in return was Michael's unqualified support at a medical board hearing. Seems Amanda was trying to get his license revoked after Peter tried to kill her. What a spoilsport!

THE BIG MERMAID

Jo and Amanda continued to vie for the attention of Jake, *Melrose's* sensitive, but often word-deprived hunk. The competition was suddenly over when a weary Jo told Amanda she was backing off. Jake was Amanda's— lock, stock, and beefcake.

Jake had only one request—to be let off the relationship merry-go-round. He headed to the quiet solitude of his boat, *The Pretty Lady*, inherited from Reed, but his Garbo fantasy never materialized. On the first night, his hermit's nest was invaded by a young woman splashing about in obvious distress. Gallant Jake dragged her aboard, where she introduced herself as Brittany Maddocks. She breathlessly explained that she was escaping the clutches of her abusive and powerful husband.

Jake's offer to get her to a telephone at the marina was met with reluctance. Although he wanted nothing more than to avoid getting trapped in her troubles, Jake turned softhearted and agreed to let her camp out on the boat for a few days.

Curvy Brittany seemed more than ready to demonstrate her gratitude with a smooch, but Jake held the eager lady at arm's length. Eventually the drip, drip, drip of her amorous offers wore him down and they danced the horizontal tango.

To Jake, the sex was a pleasurable, if meaningless, little frolic. But Big Britt obviously had more than nookie on her mind when she quickly scampered off to report her conquest to her partner in crime, Amanda's father, Palmer Woodward. They agreed they were on their way to cornering Jake. A festival of whispered arrangements and knowing winks ensued.

Meanwhile, Daddy Dearest surprised Amanda at her front door. Even his loyal daughter had trouble putting on a happy face, since the F.B.I. had trailed her while trying to nab him, following his surprise dash out of town. Not to worry, Palmer assured Amanda, he was ready to turn himself in as soon as he settled a few minor matters. Reluctantly, she agreed to let him hide out at her place.

Shaking his head to clear out his lust-induced fog, Jake reminded himself that he wanted to be alone and stayed solo at his apartment. Sensing Brittany's loosening grip on Jake, Palmer insisted she speed up the plans before the whole mess fell apart. She was soon scurrying around the boat laying wires and taping up plastique bombs.

Brittany drew the line at attempting to forge Amanda's signature, so Palmer—the scum—scammed his own daughter to continue his revenge on Jake. Insisting to Amanda that he had kept his safe deposit box a secret from her only to shield the funds from ex-wife Hillary, he pleaded with Amanda for help in withdrawing the remaining money. A bitter Amanda soon caught on to Palmer's manipulation and lost no time ringing up the F.B.I.

But it looked like poor Jake's goose was already cooked. Palmer locked horns with Jake on the boat, with Brittany as backup on a getaway Sea Ray alongside them. Their guns, pointed straight at his ticker, persuaded Jake this was no social call. Palmer planned to assume a new identity, armed with fake I.D. and a cool million, but Brittany pulled a double cross and popped him dead in the heart. She begged Jake to run away with her; he told her to go to hell without him. The angry jiltee roared off on the Sea Ray, just as Jake caught sight of the deadly wires crisscrossing his craft. A safe distance away, a crazed Brittany detonated the bombs as a fiery farewell.

After fishing a near-dead Jake out of the water, the coast guard got the details about Palmer's cruise to Davy Jones's locker. Later, Jake consoled Amanda about her father's sorry end. A stoic yet resentful daughter poured her heart out to her now silent father at the morgue. Jake's comforting remained strictly nonsexual, much to Amanda's frustration.

YOU DON'T KNOW ME, BUT...

Jake could do no right—even a pregnant and lonely Jo resented his shrugging her off to comfort Amanda. At the end of his emotional rope, he turned his apartment keys over to Matt and bolted off down the freeway.

Feeling lost, Jake had decided the time had come to find his real father, Vince Conners. His startled dad (it was only a one-night-stand, after all) tried to buy him off with dollars, which made no sense to Jake. Any fantasy he had of forming a genuine bond evaporated as Vince's discomfort escalated. Jake thought he'd have to resign himself to a fatherless future, but in the end Vince reassured his son that he had often wondered what had become of the proud football player whose photo he carried in his wallet. They agreed to stay in touch.

Jake returned to L.A., where an F.B.I. windfall awaited him as a reward for closing the Palmer Woodward affair. He found the perfect use for his loot—he bought Shooters. With Sydney as his sidekick/waitress, the joint started jumpin'.

Jake came to Syd's rescue when sleazy Chris Marchette, Jane's business partner, attacked her late one night. Suddenly, Jake began to see a kinder, gentler, saner side of Sydney. He chivalrously defended her honor by bashing Chris in the mouth and sending him careening into the pool. As a result, an unexpected sexual yearning arose between Sydney and Jake. They indulged it.

When Jake was muscled by a protection racket, it was Sydney who agreed to sleep with whomever she had to in order to get him off the hook. Imagine her disgust when yucky Chris Marchette met Syd at the hotel room.

KISSES AND CHEMO

Amanda and Michael began a relationship of another ilk entirely when he treated her for Hodgkin's disease. Kimberly's scar started to split when Michael accompanied his patient on a trip to New York to explore an experimental new treatment program. The two ended up sharing the only room available at their hotel (thanks to a well-placed phone call from Michael before they arrived). Doctorly concern bloomed into fervent kisses, catching Amanda at her most vulnerable and grabbing Michael unexpectedly by his normally hard-to-find heartstrings.

Michael knew that he had to solve the Kimberly-quandry after she threatened to throw a lamp into a Jacuzzi where he and Amanda were soaking and sloshing. Kimberly took his request for a divorce kinda hard—she downed a handful of pills and jiggerful of alcohol, leaving a suicide note for her hubby. When he discovered her lifeless body, he went to call 9-1-1—and then he stopped. Better to become a widower than a thrice-divorced man, Mikey mused. Pouring himself a stiff drink, he sat back and waited patiently.

But it was bad timing for him when Sydney strolled in. Seeing her seeing him, Michael burst into action, as though he had just found his unconscious wife. While he dialed for an ambulance, Syd promptly pocketed the suicide note, knowing it would be helpful in setting Michael up later. A recovered Kimberly was distraught to learn that her brush with

Asked to comment on the ethical issues regarding Dr. Peter Burns, a surgeon, treating Kimberly Shaw and having her live in his home during treatment, Dr. Edward Frischholz, a consulting and clinical psychologist in Chicago, offered the following analysis:

Why would a surgeon be practicing psychiatry or clinical psychology without any training? Why would any court or psychiatric facility allow him to?

And in this case, one wonders what lack of common sense would lead a surgeon to treat a woman with a history of violent behavior. Although a patient will idealize her therapist for helping her, almost always that honeymoon ends when she realizes that the therapist is merely human and makes mistakes like everyone else. Patients less violent than Kimberly can become aggressive and angry; given her past deeds, Dr. Burns (and his property) could be in danger.

Allowing his patient to live with him makes one question whether he intends to cultivate a sexual relationship with her. Not ethical; not wise. Besides, would she consent freely to having sex with him, or feel pressured given his power over her freedom? Or, if *she* pursues *him* sexually, he is vulnerable as well.

Other manipulations may arise. Would Dr. Burns condone Kimberly continuing to act out against her—or his—enemies, a long parade of ex-girlfriends and ex-spouses?

Frankly, I'd advise the good doctor to stick with his scalpel and leave the head shrinking to somebody else.

death had not improved her standing with Michael. And she wondered where the hell her suicide note had ended up. (She also wondered if Michael had picked up her dry cleaning, but that's another story.)

Going back on the offensive, Kimberly connived to frame Michael with attempted murder. Ever helpful, Sydney agreed to plant Seconal tablets among Kimberly's vitamins for a cool $50,000. A busy Sydney next met with Michael and offered to return the suicide note to him—getting him off the murder rap—for another $50,000. Having no choice other than strangulation, he folded. Syd used the money to buy Mancini Designs and install herself as president. Jane later ousted her.

Michael proposed to Amanda, even dropping to his knees and begging—a most unusual posture for Dr. Mancini. He failed to sway her. Amanda's good humor dried up and Michael's every move toward her was perceived as harassment, not love. Like Jane had the year before, she acquired a restraining order compelling him to keep his distance.

Pregnant by her dead drug-dealing lover Reed, Jo drifted along in a semi-shocked state. Her problems mounted when Reed's parents, Marilyn and Dennis Carter, appeared at her doorstep, asking for mementos of their departed son. Though they approached her with kindness, Jo was uncomfortable. Jake counseled her to get rid of the creep's stuff, and so she finally gave them a few of Reed's things that she'd been saving for the baby.

But women can't fool other women for long. Mrs. Carter guessed that Jo was expecting, and even surmised that Reed was the father. Relieved to unburden her secret, Jo assured the Carters that she wanted her baby to know and love his grandparents.

After this warm and fuzzy encounter, Jo was stunned to be served with legal papers from the Carters, demanding custody of her unborn child. Though she had a meager bank balance, Jo was able to hire a lawyer by selling to his firm all movie, book, and other entertainment rights to her case. The attorney, Mr. Waxman, advised her to line up character witnesses who could testify about her fitness to be a mother. But when the trial date was moved up before her due date, Jo's fears intensified.

On the stand, the opposing counsel made mincemeat of Jo's unstable stable of friends on cross-examination. The judge awarded sole custody of the baby to the Carters, effective upon his birth.

Another crisis arose for Jo when Kimberly, infertile and in the throes of baby lust, turned her laserlike attention to Jo with a scheme to "help." According to Kimberly, if she induced Jo's labor at the beach house, then brought her to the hospital, she could record the event as a stillbirth and Jo could leave town with her baby, avoiding the court order. Jo gave birth to a son, Austin.

The plan unfolded as arranged, with Kimberly substituting blood type and other data concerning Austin onto the authentic stillbirth records of another baby, named Cortes. Unfortunately, when Jo returned to the beach house to claim her child, Kimberly kept the doors locked tight. Without legal rights to her own son and with documents altered to suggest he wasn't even alive, Jo had been snookered out of her snookums a second time.

While Kimberly blissfully breastfed Jo's son (how? how? how?) and fed Michael cockamamie stories about where the bundle of joy had come from, Matt researched the hospital records to corroborate Jo's claim. Jo told Peter about Kimberly's wild ride, and he forced Michael to return the baby to his mother. Kimberly tore up the house when she realized what had happened, but, hey, the maid was coming the next day.

Marcia Cross

LADY MACBETH IN A LAB COAT

When Kimberly Shaw first came into the sights of *Melrose* devotees in her physician's togs, few knew what evil lurked beneath that doctorly demeanor. From her initial steamy clinches with fellow medicine man Michael Mancini, Kimberly's fiery-eyed ruthlessness gained a startling momentum that literally exploded the apartment complex by the end of the third season.

As Kimberly, Marcia Cross brings an impressive classical training to her distressed doctor role. At the age of seventeen, she received a scholarship to the Juilliard School in New York, and used her training to segue seamlessly from Shakespeare to soap opera. *Merchant of Venice, Two Gentlemen of Verona*, and *Twelfth Night* make up her classical repertoire. But she also appeared on two daytime dramas—as Liz Corell on *The Edge of Night* (for the show's final six months on the air) in 1984, and as anthropologist Kate Sanders on ABC's *One Life to Live*. In addition, Cross romped through a *Cheers* episode as the sexy sister of Rebecca Howe, yukked it up as Garry's Shandling's girlfriend in *It's Garry Shandling's Show*, and gave stomachaches to boyfriend James Spader in the 1990 feature film *Bad Influence*.

Cross grew up as the middle of three sisters in Marlboro, Massachusetts, and focused her baby blues on an acting career while still in elementary school. Her determination has enabled her to treat stage, daytime, nighttime, and film jobs equally, without ranking the work on a snob-o-meter. Making back-from-the-dead Kimberly believable when she whips off her wig and scaring the pants off a pants-less

Michael with her wicked scar was no mean feat. Somehow, her embodiment of Kimberly suspends our disbelief—competent physician, scheming sex kitten in red satin panties, or pathetic psychiatric patient, we buy the whole package. As Cross explained to *Entertainment Weekly*, "At one point, I was like, 'There's no way I can play this and not be the worst actress in Hollywood.' But then I decided that it was Kimberly's party, and to just play it scene-by-scene. And everybody seems to be having a blast with the character."

Her wickedness and vulnerability coexist then—if not peacefully. The root of Kimberly's evil was finally revealed when she had to face the music for blowing up the entire apartment complex. (Blame it on Henry, the gardener she stabbed when he raped her mother.) But even as Kimberly is redeemed, you get the feeling that Cross will be laughing (and scaring us to death) all the way to the end.

A nanny, Emily, seemed like the answer to Jo's prayers for some normalcy and calm in her life. But Jo's daytime nightmares started up again when Emily, in cahoots with the Carters, sped away in Jo's car with the baby. Instead of heading off to New York as she'd planned, Jo hunted down the Carters with Jake's help. Grandpa Carter wasn't about to give Austin back without a fight, however, and the trigger-happy grandpa shot Jo.

After her recovery at the hospital, a pensive and sad Mama Reynolds concluded that her son would fare better in life if she gave him up for adoption. She bid her son a teary goodbye.

DAYS OF WHINE AND ROSES

Alison's life was full of surprises—who should end up at an adjoining D&D cubicle but Billy? Seemed he'd gotten caught up in a little conflict of interest with *Escapade* and D&D; after writing a pitch letter that Amanda had used to nab the magazine's advertising biz, he was given the boot, since spilling secrets is a corporate no-no. Alison wasn't too sure she liked the idea of working alongside the man she'd stood up twice (so far).

Eager-beaver assistant Elisabeth, a newly-minted Harvard graduate, hung on Billy's every word. And, as far as Alison could tell, she did all Billy's work, but tossed Alison's requests in the circular file. After Alison complained about her uneven job performance, Lizzie was fired on the spot by Amanda. Billy was miffed.

Alison didn't care too much about Billy's bruised ego, however. At Shooters, she had met a dreamy architect named Mitch who swept her off her feet. Our little Ali-Cat slept with him, smugly thrilled that her life was moving beyond Billy. But when Mitch stood her up the next night, Alison got the last word by going to his office and dousing him with a pitcher of water.

Next on Billy's female hit parade was Alison's old friend Susan. Since Billy had moved into a different apartment at the complex, Alison invited Susan, an aspiring chef, to room with her. She had no idea that Susan would end up making Billy a special dish on her menu.

As Billy and Susan got closer, Alison got drunker. She perpetually bounced back and forth between ordering Susan to move out and begging her to stay. Events reached a fever pitch when a soused Alison instigated a messy food fight at a D&D business party catered by Susan. (How she managed to hold onto her job after that fiasco, we'll never know). Not long afterwards, Meredith, Alison's sister, came to L.A. and tried to seduce Billy. She failed.

At another D&D event, Alison stumbled upon party boy and music maven Zach Philips, who was only too happy to indulge in endless drinking bouts with her. Their binges culminated in a blackout on the beach the night before Alison was to testify on Jo's behalf at her custody hearing. After Zach gave Alison some pills to perk her up after their all-night debacle, a pooped-out Parker wasn't allowed to take the stand for her friend.

Alison finally bottomed out when she hit a young boy riding his bike. DUI charges followed, and loyal Billy used his vacation funds to bail her out. When he watched her belly up to the bar, first thing after returning home from jail, he knew he had to make her face her alcoholism. A hastily-organized confrontation with Billy, Susan, and Matt convinced Alison to enter a treatment program at Twin Oaks Rehab Center.

While drying out (and eating bad institutional grub), Alison began a romance with Terry Parsons, a professional football player and recovering sex and alcohol addict. Billy was jealous of Terry and Alison's intimacy; Terry couldn't cope with Billy's constant, curly-haired presence. Though Alison and Terry enjoyed many glamorous events after leaving rehab, including a trip to a pro football game, their mini-engagement shorted out when she realized sobriety was the only thing they had in common.

Back at the office, Alison and Billy worked hard to cover for Amanda during her battle with cancer. Alison tried valiantly to hold onto the Franklin Cruises account, even spilling the beans on the sly about Amanda's illness. Unfortunately, that little maneuver almost resulted in the client firing D&D. Alison hid under her copy of *Advertising Age* after that one.

AM I MY BROTHER'S KILLER?

At Shooters, the phone jingled with nerve-jangling news—Jake's mother, Stella, had died. Even more disturbing was the prospect of seeing his older half-brother Jess. With Jo in tow, Jake journeyed up to Washington state for the funeral. Unfortunately, the bad blood between the boys wasn't buried as swiftly as their mother's cold corpse. Jess resented—loudly—bearing the brunt of their mother's drunken excesses. Jo encouraged Jake to make peace.

Next thing Jake knew, Jess had abandoned his trailer home for the bright lights of Los Angeles. Jake reluctantly gave him a job at Shooters. But Sydney knew a snake when it hissed, and took note of Jess's casual ransacking of Jake's ledgers.

Thomas Calabro

Though Dr. Michael Mancini lives in a beach house perched at the edge of the Pacific, Thomas Calabro is pure "New Yawk," born in Brooklyn and raised in Queens. Life in the Calabro clan was always tight-knit. Even as a football-playing high schooler, Calabro

pitched in with his brother and sister at their pop's neighborhood luncheonette as a short order cook. "It was good, in retrospect," he shared with *TV Guide*. "But at the time, I really hated it."

College drew Calabro no further than Fordham University in the Bronx, where the class of '81 grad was still enticed more by the fifty-yard line than the classroom. When he didn't survive the team cut early on, Calabro enrolled in a school-sponsored summer stock program associated with Lincoln Center in Manhattan. That apprenticeship, and a season with the Actors Lab, cured him of his Brooklyn bray and put gas in his acting tank.

Following graduation, Calabro spent a number of years as a performer and director in such diverse productions as *Sweet Basil*, *Open Admissions*, and *Wild Blue*, an acting extravaganza of eight vignettes that featured him in seven parts. But vignettes can't make the Visa payments, so Calabro lathered up for a *Zest* commercial and appeared in such choice television bits as Peter Falk's nephew on *Columbo: No Time to Die* (with a best buddy played by, of all people, Doug Savant). In 1988, he jiggled through an embarrassing TV movie role in *Lady Killers* as a cop who *really* goes undercover—all the way down to his skivvies—as a male stripper. Well, that's one way to catch a serial killer.

When he first auditioned for *Melrose Place*, Calabro wanted to read for Billy, whose storyline he felt had more pizzazz than Michael's. But because Calabro was already past thirty, the producers insisted he was too old to play a realistic Billy Campbell. So Dr. Mancini it was.

Having survived the first year as part of the show's dullest duo (together with Josie Bissett), Calabro danced in the streets when the good doc became the show's leading, sex-soaked troublemaker. As the actor told *Rolling Stone*, "The whole thing evolved nicely. I guess what happened was that the writers were getting to know all of us. [awkward pause] I'm *never* going to live that down."

Happy to serve up whatever demented plots the writers dish out, Calabro has learned that in *Melrose* reality, it's wiser not to ask "why?" "The style of the show is 'Do not question and do not allow the audience time to question,'" he admitted to *Entertainment Weekly*.

And let's face it—turning Michael Mancini into a bad guy has made Calabro a familiar (if sometimes disliked) face. "On a plane to Toronto," Calabro told *People* "someone sent me a napkin with 'How could you do that to Jane?' scrawled across it."

Off camera, Calabro is a mellow married man, head over heels for wife Elisabeth, a writer, and their year-old daughter, Conner Shea. Between his husband-hood, watching reruns of *The Brady Bunch*, and hitting the links on the golf course, Calabro's real life shows no sign of resemblance to his hormonally challenged alter ego.

This year, Calabro was the first of the cast to direct an episode, giving him a chance to exercise the directing muscles he developed during numerous New York stage productions (including a play called *Orphans*, which was performed at various homeless shelters around Manhattan). And he's also intent on spreading his wings beyond the Fox lot—last fall, he played a kidnapper in the CBS movie *Stolen Innocence*. Say, Dr. Mancini hasn't kidnapped anyone yet, has he?

Jess concentrated all his limited charms on Jo, much to Jake's annoyance. At a three-way-J dinner—Jake, Jess, and Jo—Jess insisted on picking up the tab. Jake wondered how a bankrupt lowlife like his brother could get a credit card—easily, it seems, since he had palmed one when a Shooters' customer left it behind. Jo ping-ponged between her rash fascination with Jess and guilty devotion to Jake. Lust won out in Jo's darkroom when she and Jess exposed more than film.

Jake responded by firing Jess and kicking him out of the apartment. But Jess made up his mind—he wanted Jake's woman and Jake's business, so he hired a hit man, Butch, to pick off his brother. Butch did the dirty deed at Shooters. Hanson hit the silent alarm—but it was too late. Jake had been shot.

Though Jess played innocent with Jo, she took the incident as a sign and called off their affair. Jess balked, but went along with her decision. Playing the concerned brother role to the hilt, Jess showed up at Shooters and rehired himself to keep the bar open, much to Sydney and Jake's suspicious disgust. But Jo melted like butter on a hot griddle and took Jess back.

When Jake returned to Shooters, he kicked Jess out of the place for good. To keep him off his back, however, Jake wrangled him a construction job at a high-rise site.

At a scenic lookout, Jess proposed to Jo, who held him off. But like a dog with a bone, he would not let up on the marriage issue. Back at the apartment, their "discussion" turned nasty. Jess viciously beat Jo into submission and jammed the engagement ring onto her finger.

Jake discovered a whimpering Jo crawling onto the apartment landing and instantly tore off in a frenzy to confront Jess at the construction site. The brothers fought atop a high scaffold, and tumbled over the edge. It was impossible to tell if either one had survived.

UNLUCKY IN LOVE

While out jogging, Matt was surprised to run into his former sailor/lover, Jeffrey. Though he'd resigned from the service and returned to L.A., Jeff had held off reestablishing contact with Matt because of his H.I.V. positive diagnosis.

Matt agonized about getting involved with Jeffrey again—and continued to change his mind every time Michael offered his perplexing opinions. Ultimately, it was Jeff who called it quits.

Kimberly and Matt continued their longstanding cat-and-mouse game. Things turned mean when she hired thugs to beat him up in retaliation for not changing the results of her psychiatric evaluation. While reporting the incident to the police, Matt met Jonathan, a sympathetic gay cop.

Jonathan agreed to take Jo on a ride-along to help her prepare for a photo shoot of street gangs. While on patrol with him, Jo took incriminating photos of him mercilessly beating a drug suspect. When the suspect later died, Jo and Matt hemmed and hawed about what to do with the revealing pictures. Things turned ugly when her camera equipment was stolen, prompting Matt to turn the photos over to the police. When Jonathan saw Matt at the station, he feared he'd been betrayed and later held Matt and Jo at gunpoint at the apartment. Jo, tired of being victimized, grabbed the weapon from the rogue cop while Matt called in backup.

Matt was sure his romantic luck was on the upswing when he met Paul Graham, a plastic surgeon at the hospital. Paul confided that he was in the process of extricating himself from an unhappy marriage. He begged Matt to be patient, but all the last-minute broken dates gave Matt a bad headache. At home, Paul convinced his wife Carolyn that Matt was stalking them, leading her to threaten Matt to keep away from her husband.

Events ran amuck when Paul told Matt that Carolyn was leaving town. If he wanted to, suggested Paul, Matt could go to his home and begin cooking an intimate feast for the two of them. Paul promised Matt that the burglar alarm system would be turned off, but he was as fake as one of his nose jobs. The moment Matt unlocked the front door, bells began to ring. He phoned Paul at once. Don't worry, Paul shmoozed him, the cops'll be right over to fix everything. (Why not just tell him how to turn off the damn alarm?)

Matt glanced down the hallway and spotted Carolyn lying on the floor. A close-up look revealed her bludgeoned head next to a candlestick that Matt had handled a few evenings earlier. The cops arrived, sure enough, and straightaway concluded Matt was both a burglar and a murderer.

Held in an interrogation room with the detectives, Matt reiterated his contrite tale, insisting that Paul would back him up. (Sure, just like Kimberly did for Sydney.) Imagine Matt's astonishment when the cops revealed that the Grahams had filed harassment complaints against him. Matt began to realize he'd been set up when Paul himself arrived and lunged at him, screaming that Matt had murdered his beloved wife. In a fury, Matt ran at Paul, but was restrained by the cops.

Down the Aisle

Y ou are cordially invited to the weddings and near weddings of *Melrose's* favorite couples. Black tie optional.

The Bride: Katya Petrova   *The Groom:* Matt Fielding

R.S.V.P.: Doctor Katya wanted a green card so she and daughter Nikki could remain stateside. Bighearted Matt waved away her offers of money in exchange for a marriage license. They trooped down the aisle in a quiet ceremony: Katya wore a cream-colored wedding suit and cloche hat. Matt looked utterly distinguished in a dark suit and tie. The gang partied with them afterwards at a Russian restaurant. *Anniversary Report:* Hard to tell, since Katya and Nikki are back in Mother Russia. But, hey, was there ever a divorce?

The Bride: Jane Mancini   *The Groom:* Chris Marchette

R.S.V.P.: Jane almost got permanently duped by Chris. Her sleazy business partner wanted to marry her to get his hands on the cash in her corporate cookie jar. The couple flew to Las Vegas to play roulette and tie the knot, but Michael was not ready to give his ex-bride away. In the middle of the ceremony, he and Kimberly arrived to scream their objections. If you want to see what happened next, read on.

The Bride: Kimberly Shaw   *The Groom:* Michael Mancini

R.S.V.P.: It must have been something in the desert air of Las Vegas that turned Michael's heart to mush—or maybe it was the simple fact that he and Kimberly had never followed through after becoming engaged the year before—a near-fatal car accident *can* muck up the best laid plans. In any event, once Michael and Kimberly made sure that Chris and Jane didn't swap "I do's," they decided to take the plunge themselves. *Anniversary Report:* What anniversary? Quicker than you can say "community property," Michael threatened to file for divorce since the only thing fertile about Kimberly was her imagination. But with these two, never say never. Their passion runs hot and cold, so the marriage may linger on.

The Bride: Sydney Andrews   *The Groom:* A Reluctant Michael Mancini

R.S.V.P.: Unfortunately, all "no's." This match made in blackmail heaven kept the guests away. Livid sister Jane caught sight of Syd in the family heirloom lace gown and redesigned it as a "wet look" with a quick dunk in the pool. Sydney had her lonely way, and married Michael on the beach. *Anniversary Report:* When his fiancée, Kimberly, returned from the dead, Michael ditched his wife.

The Bride: Alison Parker   *The Groom:* Billy Campbell

R.S.V.P.: This was *MP's* biggest wedding that wasn't. The whole gang—even black-hearted Amanda—had gathered around the complex's flower bedecked pool. Billy was more than ready in his tux; moments before the vows, however, Alison doffed her traditional froufrou frock and defenestrated. Papa Parker knew why she bolted, but kept his lips zipped. Billy was left holding the bouquet and an awful lot of stuffed mushrooms.

The Bride: Brooke Armstrong   *The Groom:* Billy Campbell

R.S.V.P.: As soon as dilettante debutante Brooke locked her big brown eyes on Billy, she was heard murmuring, "Mmm, mmm, that's for me!" Alison was a mere impediment; Daddy Hayley's disapproval a minor annoyance—she had to bag that boy. At Hayley's sumptuous Pasadena digs she sashayed past the throng in a satiny haltered gown and gauntlet gloves. Alison winged it back from Hong Kong in time to make a bedraggled fool of herself, but Billy turned his morning-coated back on her and pledged his troth. *Anniversary Report:* Let's see. . .a pretend pregnancy, a suicide attempt . . . it's all water down the pool drain now, since Brooke's gone bye-bye permanently.

The Bride: Alison Parker   *The Groom:* Hayley Armstrong

R.S.V.P.: After all those botched attempts at marrying Billy, Alison blithely tied the knot with older, richer, and very adorable Hayley Armstrong. The wedding had extra sizzle, since Hayley was Brooke's father—and Brooke's husband was, of course Billy! After dropping to his knees to pop the question (in front of Mr. and Mrs. Campbell, no less), Hayley got Alison to say yes. They did the deed in Rosarita Beach, Mexico, surrounded by dozens of candles—and no witnessess. *Anniversary Report:* Could Hayley get used to eating pizza three nights a week? Will Alison get a full set of keys to all her husband's locked rooms? Is a wedding legal if there are no witnesses? Does any of this matter if the husband jumps overboard and dies?

Jane found herself with non-refundable reservations for a short stay in the pokey as the first suspect in the attempted murder of Michael. Her Australian business acquaintance Chris Marchette bailed her out, and the charges against her were dropped when she fingered sister Sydney, who had better motive and opportunity, let alone Jane's car and apartment keys.

Jane and Chris found the growing sexual magnetism between them harder and harder to brush aside. Sydney, working at Mancini Designs on probation, saw through Chris's pleasant veneer to the muck underneath, but Jane dismissed her senseless sister's judgment.

Chris continued to insinuate himself into Jane's professional life by conning her into a joint business checking account for their "convenience." On the personal front, she was confused by his reluctance to sleep with her, in spite of his obvious interest. His chivalrous behavior both puzzled and pleased her.

Perhaps if Jane had heard the obscene phone calls Chris made to Sydney she'd have greater insight into his kinky proclivities. Chris revealed himself to Sydney as her unwanted caller during an ill-fated birthday bash in her honor. Syd told Jane that Chris was a freak, but Jane refused to believe her.

On a pleasure trip to Las Vegas, Chris gambled and won big, a turn-on so huge for him that he attacked Jane in a rush of rough sex that carried none of the emotional tenderness she wanted. Refusing to think above the waist, Jane decided to marry Chris while in Vegas. Michael was afraid that his financial interest in Mancini Designs would be endangered if Jane and Chris tied the knot, so he and Kimberly hotfooted it to the Strip. They put the kibosh on the ceremony—and ended up getting married themselves.

Back at Mancini Designs, Chris and Jane maintained their professional partnership, waiting to get hitched at a later time. Chris had more pressing matters to manhandle, like cashing Jane's hard earned $500,000 line of credit. With the money, he kidnapped Sydney to Las Vegas to indulge her on a grand scale. A startled Syd was instantly smitten with the diamond necklace Chris casually draped around her neck in the limo, and the endless luxuries he heaped upon her at their Caesar's Palace hotel suite.

The materially-deprived Sydney couldn't resist the lush life—up to a point. When she learned Chris had gambled—and lost—Jane's business funds, she got on the horn and called Jake to rescue her. A posse of Jake, Jane, and Michael was baffled by the radiant state of the victim when they rescued Sydney from captivity.

A chastened Jane grabbed at another chance to fulfill her design dreams by approaching Richard Hart of Mackenzie Hart Designs. His basically loveless marriage to his older designer-wife Mackenzie was held together by the unraveling threads of professional success. Jane vamped Richard and won a job with the company that allowed her to create an original line. A steamed Mackenzie watched helplessly as the young beauty stole her husband's heart away.

TAKE HER TO YOUR LEADER

Sydney was back in a bad financial hole when Amanda upped the rent. Needing help, she took in a roommate, Rikki, who had some strange habits, and we're not talking about insisting that the toilet paper roll off from the top. Rikki was a member of a cult, headed by guru Martin Abbot, and correctly coined Sydney as a perfect mark. Systematically Rikki turned Syd's friends against her by ruining Jo's photography equipment, shredding Mancini gowns, and trashing Shooters—with all suspicions falling on Sydney, as usual.

Life at the rustic sect didn't suit city-girl Sydney, but her attempt to leave landed her in a locked, semi-buried box "to think it over." Luckily she discovered she was a crack shot during sharpshooting practice at the compound, which came in handy when Jane and Jake rescued her (again!). Sydney shot out all the tires on the cult's vehicles and zipped back to L.A. and her waitressing job at Shooters. Jane and Jake had a brief affair, much to Syd's disgust.

PRINCESS MACHIAVELLI

Not all Alison's work moves were missteps. She entered and won the Advertiser of the Year Award for her Glorious Gowns campaign, to Amanda's peroxided disgust. The D&D board rewarded Alison with the company's presidency, and fired Amanda.

Once named top dog, Alison exhibited a ruthlessness that would have made Genghis Khan proud. Whether harshly commandeering her troops or wickedly pinning Billy to her desk for some torrid, mindless sex, the girl sank her claws into every available soft surface. Even her cheerleader, eager intern Brooke Armstrong, soon switched sides and began feeding information to Amanda, who was plotting her eventual return to the throne.

Patrick Muldoon

Patrick Muldoon has that undefinable "It." The guy has so much magnetism—on screen and off—that in 1995 television guru Aaron Spelling handpicked him to be the future centerpiece of a new Spelling series. In the meantime, he's presented Muldoon with the character of *Melrose's* Richard Hart to keep him happy. And Muldoon's loving it. Throw in the fact that the California native is one of the friendliest, down-to-earth actors you could ever want to meet, and visions of success on the level of Brad Pitt start swimming before your eyes. The ex-Calvin Klein model first became familiar to television viewers as hunky Austin Reed on the soap *Days of Our Lives* in 1992. Austin, from the wrong side of the tracks, but with a heart of gold, promptly won over a gaggle of fans and kept them panting for more. Muldoon's dashing good looks made a career in acting a natural choice, though it was actually football that was his original goal.

As an undergrad, Muldoon played tight end at the University of Southern California at Los Angeles. But when he realized that the odds of becoming a professional player were slim, he redrew his game plan, and acting soon became his first pick. A recurring role on *Who's the Boss?* together with appearances on *Silk Stalkings* and *Saved By the Bell* cemented his choice. But even now, Muldoon sees his acting future in strictly sports terms. "It all goes back to football. The pecking order, the depth chart, first string, second string. You just have to keep working up that ladder," he told *Entertainment Weekly.*

Perhaps Muldoon's pragmatism stems from his very grounded upbringing. Mom is an artist, Dad's a lawyer. He still remains close to his sister, Shayna, eight years his junior. When he's not working, Muldoon counts playing sports (no surprise) and music among his favorite activities.

Melrose has already made Muldoon into meaty tabloid fodder. While their relationship is *not* romantic, the rags have made much of his friendship with Tori Spelling (*Beverly Hills 90210*'s Donna, and Aaron's real-life daughter). The pair did attend the 1995 prime-time Emmy Awards together, and appeared in the 1996 television movie, *Deadly Pursuits,* but it's not a love match, kiddies.

Whether Muldoon's deep blue eyes can kick his career into the stratosphere remains to be seen. But you can just bet that he'll still pick up his own dry cleaning.

When Brooke's mind wasn't on aiding and abetting Amanda, she was aggressively luring an oblivious Billy into her lair. Though supposedly engaged to a fop named Lowell, Brooke's wealthy background fed her air of entitlement—whatever she wanted, she got. And her father, zillionaire businessman Hayley, made sure her every wish came true. Their intimacy skirted the edge of decency, though it never crossed the line.

In a moment of underhanded charity, Alison rehired Amanda for a low-paying, low status position. Amanda seized her opportunity, and she and Brooke schemed to embarrass Alison with the Mrs. Molly's Cookies account. They let her devise a campaign featuring a woman diving out a window, knowing all the while the client would balk, since his mother had jumped to her death.

Alison didn't remain clueless forever, and enlisted Brooke to spy on Amanda. Brooke reveled in her double-agent status. But as her interest in Billy increased, Brooke decided it was necessary to get Alison completely out of his sight in order to hook him. Alison inadvertently helped out by being ousted after the Mrs. Molly's debacle. Brooke's father, Hayley "saved the day" by offering Alison a cushy job in Hong Kong.

Billy finally succumbed to Brooke's relentless charms, and proposed to her. Hayley had been hoping for a more refined mate for his little darling and made no bones about Billy's shortcomings, right to Billy's face. Hayley's thinly-veiled threats—that Billy's chances of survival would be nil if he didn't keep Brooke-baby happy—didn't scare off the groom-to-be.

A lonely Alison called back to the States, reaching Amanda at the office. Gee, are you calling to congratulate the happy couple? Amanda sweetly asked. Alarmed at the sudden nuptials, Alison hopped a plane to stop the ceremony. After nailbiting delays, she limped to the wedding a wrinkled, blue-jeaned mess. Alison begged Billy to give their relationship another chance, but her pleas fell on deaf ears—although it was a good side show for the well-heeled guests. Defeated, tired, and alone, Alison returned to her Melrose digs, blasted the stereo, and took a long pull of vodka.

SOLDIER GIRL

Meanwhile, Kimberly hied herself off to a feminist paramilitary training boot camp, *No More Victims*, in order to regain her confidence. Back in L.A., she appeared to make amends with Michael, Amanda, and others with whom she'd crossed swords. However, her true intention was to wreak havoc on an atomic scale. And she wasn't alone in these efforts; every time she looked into the mirror, the demented grimace of her psychotic alter image, "Henry," leered back at her. Henry persisted in fueling her paranoid fantasies, finally convincing her that a mass bombing of the apartment complex would be just revenge. (More on Kimberly's disarming logic later.)

Michael sensed trouble and enlisted Sydney's help. When she stumbled upon Kimberly's sicko shrine to her enemies, complete with photographs featuring gouged-out eyes, she knew the whole gang was in big trouble.

BOMBS AWAY!

A fragile Kimberly leaned further over the edge when she watched Peter shmooze Michael and Sydney at the Beverly Hills Physican Association's cocktail party following his successful board hearing. Though she was happy that Peter had kept his medical license, his zealous pursuit of reinstatement at Wilshire Memorial left her lonely. Shoved out his door when she was hoping for a little lovemaking, Kimberly became enraged when she heard Peter leaving a message on Amanda's answering machine. By sending a fake note from Amanda along with a bottle of champagne, Kimberly lured Peter into her bomb-laden trap at the apartment complex.

More lives were in danger at the complex, also: Billy had forgotten the plane tickets for his honeymoon, so he and Brooke were there; Jane and Richard were making love, and Mackenzie had come over to make trouble for them.

Syd found Kimberly, but she should have brought backup. By threat of blowtorch, Kimberly forced Syd to call Michael—after all, the bombing would be a bust if *his* hind end wasn't blown sky high, too. Sydney was bound and gagged once she got off the phone. Michael and the lady bomber scuffled in the basement, and at last he knocked her out. Freeing Sydney, the two of them raced upstairs to warn the unsuspecting residents to get out fast, before the place detonated into a kabillion bits.

Oh, My Stars!

BY LITTLE DIPPER

Is it any surprise, sky watchers, that those born under the stars that hover over *Melrose Place* come to us from the signs that represent sex and passion, glamour, bitchy repartee, and overheated drama? As they doff their breakaway blouses, measure their biceps, connive, and stomp away from each other, we are watching some of the most potent signs of the zodiac clash. With so many impressionable and air signs represented, it's no wonder that *Melrose Place* has become the latest rage. The complete absence of earth signs in this cast would indicate that this is not an especially grounded crowd, obsessed with security and long-term planning.

ARIES (March 21 - April 20)
Marcia Cross — MARCH 25

Impulsive, impatient, and in-your-face, Aries are the natural leaders of the zodiac. Known for their athletic skills and explosive temperaments, they can be relentless when pursuing their goals, arguing a point or launching a romance. They like their independence and will not tolerate possessive ploys from lovers or friends. They believe rules are made to be broken, especially if they're breaking them. You may recognize the Aries native by a prominent head.

GEMINI (May 22–June 21)
Doug Savant — JUNE 21

Clever, biting and lighter than popcorn, Geminis are quick, highly impressionable, curious folks who possess keen intellects, but may have trouble focusing because they're too busy chatting, vacillating and otherwise avoiding decisions. Some people think they possess a dual nature; others just think they're two-faced. They excel in communications and can handle many projects—or love affairs—simultaneously. Their own feelings confuse them, so don't expect them to spend any time worrying about yours.

LEO (July 24–August 23)

Laura Leighton — JULY 24

Drama queens and kings, Leos arrive on stage ready to take over. A regal and highly creative sign, Leos lead lavish, exuberant, attention-getting lives (Madonna). If you bore them, you might as well be wallpaper. If you disrespect them, expect nothing less than exile. Leos seldom lose heart when something—or someone—arouses their interest. They can be pathetically stubborn, suckers for flattery, and loyal to a fault.

LIBRA (September 24 - October 23)

Heather Locklear — SEPTEMBER 25
Patrick Muldoon — SEPTEMBER 27
Jack Wagner — OCTOBER 3
Josie Bissett — OCTOBER 5

With all the attitude bouncing around the zodiac, the cosmos needs someone to pave the rocky road and bring estranged parties into accord. That's why we have Librans. Diplomatic and decorous, they hate messes—like your kitchen table—and dread any unpleasant personal confrontation. Their strong sense of social justice will turn them into activists, though. Eminently sophisticated and good-looking—like Heather and Josie, the women are frequently beautiful—these mild souls are far more ambitious than most people realize.

SCORPIO (October 24–November 22)

Daphne Zuniga — OCTOBER 28
Courtney Thorne-Smith — NOVEMBER 3

The alleged sex beasts of the zodiac, Scorpios are renowned for their passion. Whether it's directed toward fields as diverse as murder (Charles

Manson) or art (Pablo Picasso) or politics (Indira Gandhi), you're not likely to forget the results. Along the way, however, expect plenty of extremes, secrecy, and control tactics. If you ever cross them, flee now, because they will nail your sorry ass to the nearest wall. Scorpios are expert at biding their time.

AQUARIUS (January 21–February 19)

Thomas Calabro — FEBRUARY 3

Aquarians go against the grain. Sometimes they produce a genuine revolution (James Joyce); sometimes it's just demagoguery (Ronald Reagan). While they love a crowd, these charismatic cuties actually fear intimacy because they'd rather stick their hands in a bucket of clams than reveal their emotions. Consequently, they may treat your personal interest in them impersonally. Their minds are usually elsewhere anyway. But if you're looking to do something wild, they're always up for it.

PISCES (February 20–March 20)

Andrew Shue — FEBRUARY 20
Kristin Davis — FEBRUARY 23
Grant Show — FEBRUARY 27

Few have accused those born under this sign of living in the real world. Pisces are idealists; some, like David Koresh, would rather die than surrender their illusions. Ruled by Neptune, the planet of inspiration, music, and addictive behavior, Pisceans are frequently glamorous, like Liz Taylor, and may change their minds about marriage as often as she does. They can be mysterious, or just in a fog, depending on which one you get. These intuitive, sympathetic, sometimes psychic souls are naturals for charity work (they really like to Do Something), but have a tendency to practice the art of self-sacrifice too well. Be a dear friend, not a doormat.

Little Dipper is a Brooklyn-based astrologer at home in any galaxy.

Off the market now: Andrew Shue and his wife, Jennifer, who married on October 7, 1995, at Shue's Montana hideaway.

Working Stiffs

Peter wants Michael to testify on his behalf to get his medical license back.

PETER: I've got a medical board hearing at the end of the week. They want to yank my license.

MICHAEL: You're kidding. Just 'cause you tried to kill one of your patients?

———————

Jane wants Amanda to introduce her to rag businessman Richard Hart.

AMANDA: I don't think he'd be interested in the pencil scrawls of a bankrupt wannabe.

———————

But Jane corners him in an elevator and makes her pitch.

AMANDA: I must hand it to you—you aimed, you fired, you hit the bull's-eye with Richard Hart.

JANE: Some of your ruthlessness must have rubbed off on me. Good thing you have so much to spare.

———————

Michael works the room at the Physicians' Association of Beverly Hills cocktail party.

MICHAEL: Now, who here might benefit my career? Let's start with Cardiology and work our way down.

———————

Amanda visits Alison at the Twin Oaks Rehab Center.

AMANDA: So, this is Camp Happy Talk. Twelve thousand for a month of psychobabble. Too bad we couldn't write it off as severance pay.

———————

Billy sweet-talks Elisabeth, the eager new D&D assistant. Alison overhears.

BILLY: If you're new to L.A. and your name starts with a vowel, you get a free lunch on Wednesdays.

ALISON: "If you're new to L.A. and your name starts with a vowel, you get a free lunch." You used that same line on me when I first met you!

Alison ask new roommate Billy in the first season what kind of work he does.

BILLY: I'm a writer.
ALISON: Writer? What kind of writer?
BILLY: A novelist.
ALISON: You mean like Jackie Collins?
BILLY: No, I mean like Norman Mailer.

Alison's aglow when Hal Barber takes her to a D&D event while she's still a receptionist.

ALISON: Hal, thank you for bringing me. I mean, this really is amazing. It's exactly what I dreamed these parties would be.
HAL: Now, now, now, it's just a product launch for a particularly rancid flavor of wine cooler.
ALISON: I know. What can I say? I'm easily impressed.

Amanda reassures Michael she can outmaneuver Jane.

AMANDA: What can I say? When God was passing out business sense, Jane was still at the back of the line getting her nails done.

Amanda accepts congratulations from a prospective new client.

JOHN: Amanda, I have to hand it to you. You've done a very impressive sales job here. You're gonna have me signing up with D&D or running screaming from the room.
AMANDA: Well, I've locked all the doors, John. You won't get out alive.

Sydney, thinking Lauren's still in jail, tells the call girls she'll be running the show.

SYDNEY: Well, my personal life may suck, but at least I've still got a career.

———

Richard bristles at Jane's big changes to the Mackenzie-Hart line.

JANE: Lighten up, Richard. A rehash of Mack's tired old designs won't get us a spread in *Vogue*.

RICHARD: Well, that's not your call, is it?

JANE: Fine. Then you can just go into the antique clothing business and while you're at it, maybe you can bring back the bellbottom.

———

Kimberly's not too cooperative with the court-appointed psychiatrist who's testing her fitness to stand trial with some inkblots.

DOCTOR: Just tell me what you see. Whatever pops into your mind.

KIMBERLY: Okay, I see a depressed middle-aged Freudian with unexpressed homosexual leanings.

———

Brooke whines that Amanda doesn't appreciate her efforts at D&D.

AMANDA: You know, Brooke, I've had it. You claim credit you don't deserve and you blame everyone else when you can't make the grade. If it wasn't for Alison, we wouldn't have the Armstrong account. If it wasn't for me, you wouldn't even have a job.

———

Jack's lawyer wants Amanda to sign papers in the hospital room.

AMANDA: Can't it wait for a slightly more appropriate moment? Oh, sorry, I forgot, you're a lawyer.

———

Jo breaks the news to Jake that she's going to Hawaii—to work.

JO: Besides, it's only for a week—strictly business.

JAKE: Promise not to have fun.

———

Peter leaves the office for the day.

PETER: I'm going home. Can you handle any emergencies that come up tonight, Michael?

MICHAEL: I can if they have insurance.

———

Back when Peter was chief of staff and Michael a resident:

PETER: Dr. Mancini, as a resident, you're on duty 24 hours a day. You eat, you live, and you breathe the Wilshire Memorial. Now those are my rules. Play by them, or find another sandbox.

Looking cute together off-camera in 1992. Thorne-Smith: "We were two nice kids under this incredible stress. I don't know if I could have gotten through it without him."

Family Matters

Hayley wastes no time expressing his disappointment that Brooke is engaged to Billy.

> BROOKE: Billy's like that little company you bought in St. Louis. He's an undervalued asset. With the right management, he can be a Fortune 500 company in no time.

And on the wedding day, some words for Billy.

> HAYLEY: The point is, if you do anything to hurt my little girl, I'm going to take it all away from you—the job, the career, your self-respect. I have the power to bounce you from vice president to street sweeper before I've had my morning coffee. Am I making myself clear?

Then Hayley tries to insist that Billy leave for the honeymoon immediately, even though the complex was bombed.

> BILLY: You know what? You can wait until you're strapped in a wheelchair and you're spitting up your peas. But I will never, never take orders from you. And you can continue your sick relationship with your daughter as long as you want—and you'll do it without me.

Brooke cannot believe what her inheritance from her mother turns out to be.

> BROOKE: Ten thousand dollars? How the hell am I supposed to live on ten thousand dollars?

Adding insult to injury, Alison moves in with her father.

> BROOKE: Billy, she's moving into my house—my house!
> BILLY: It's your father's house, Brooke.

Jake, newly released from the hospital, is kicking Jess out of Shooters.

> JESS: If I leave now, Jake, that's it. I don't have a brother.
> JAKE: Works for me.

Jake meets his biological father, Vince.

> JAKE: I've never bothered you before—ever. All I'm asking for is a little of your time.

Vince looks uncomfortable.

> JAKE: Forget it. If you can't give me a couple hours out of your whole damn life, then I'm probably better off *not* knowing you.

Meredith's holding a gun on Dad.

> DAD: Alison, sweetheart, in spite of all this, you and Meredith turned out just fine.

Sydney can't believe Jane has told the cops she thinks Sydney mowed down Michael.

> SYDNEY: That's what you told them. To save your own stinking hide, you fingered me.

And then Daddy won't post Sydney's bail.

> SYDNEY: You think I did it? My own father thinks I tried to kill someone?. . . You don't love me. You've got Jane. You're throwing me away. Come on, Daddy, say it. Say I'm a killer.

Mrs. Parker begs her daughters to drop the lawsuits against their father.

> MOM: You two are putting a knife in my back. You're pathetic, you know that? "We have to get out the truth." Everybody lies. The world is full of it. And everybody lives with pain. But

not you two, oh no, you're going to live pure and clean by covering your parents with filth. I wish I'd never had you—either of you—I wish you'd never been born.

Michael holds Sydney off when she resists the divorce.

MICHAEL: You're not Mrs. Mancini. There's only one Mrs. Mancini, and that's my damn mother.

Jake gives Billy the Cliff Notes version of what happened between him and Jess.

JAKE: I found Jess and we fought and we fell and he died.

Matt's incensed that his parents are urging him to plea bargain out of the attempted murder charge.

MATT: Avoid what? What? Bad publicity? Is that what this is all about? Covering up this case so that nobody finds out that your son's a fruit?

Forever Felicia: Practical joker Jack Wagner gets serious with wife Kristina of *General Hospital*.

Jack Wagner

Jack Wagner likes to keep his audience guessing. He's dominated daytime television, pounded down the door of prime-time television, and topped the musical charts. Even on *Melrose Place*, viewers are never quite sure if Burns is the no-goodnik who wanted to use Amanda's appendix as a paperweight or the humanitarian who nursed Kimberly through her post-bomb trauma. You almost get the feeling that Wagner likes playing both sides. But in real life, the guy's always been a straight arrow, headed for the bull's-eye.

The acting bug first bit Wagner while he was growing up in Washington, Missouri, a small town outside of St. Louis. As a high school student, he was interested not only in theater but also in football and golf (he was a national college champion). His keen interest in the green continues to this day, as a member of the Celebrity Golf Association. And the fellow is famous for zooming off to the links every spare moment he can find.

After attending the University of Arizona in Tucson, Wagner began to pursue acting more vigorously. His crack at the big time came when he won the singing competition on *Star Search*. Music mogul Quincy Jones offered him a record deal which led to a hit single, *All I Need*, in 1985. (The tour for the record featured a then-unknown Roseanne Barr as his opening act.) Wagner went on to score one more Top Ten hit, *Lady of My Heart*, and released another album, *Lighting Up the Night*.

In 1983 he joined the daytime soap *General Hospital* as the heroic Frisco Jones. The role earned him heartthrob status and a real-life wife in 1993 when he married his costar, actress Kristina Malandro (Felicia). He went on to play Warren Lockridge on the now-defunct NBC soap, *Santa Barbara*. But along the way, Wagner has not let his singing career slide. He's appeared in several musicals, including *They're Playing Our Song*, *West Side Story*, and *Grease*. "It's a luxury to have a working wife. It allowed me to be picky and make the move to prime time," he explained to *Entertainment Weekly*.

Wagner's known on the *Melrose* set for being a good actor as well as a supreme jokester, but his outlandishness hasn't fazed anyone. "Heather [Locklear] gets me back by eating garlic like three times a day. Between us, she has horrible breath. She thinks I sweat 'cause she is hot. Wrong! It's her breath," he joked to *Entertainment Weekly*. Relax—such comments are just part of the Wagnerian charm.

The Love Web

All romantic entanglements are full-tilt boogie.

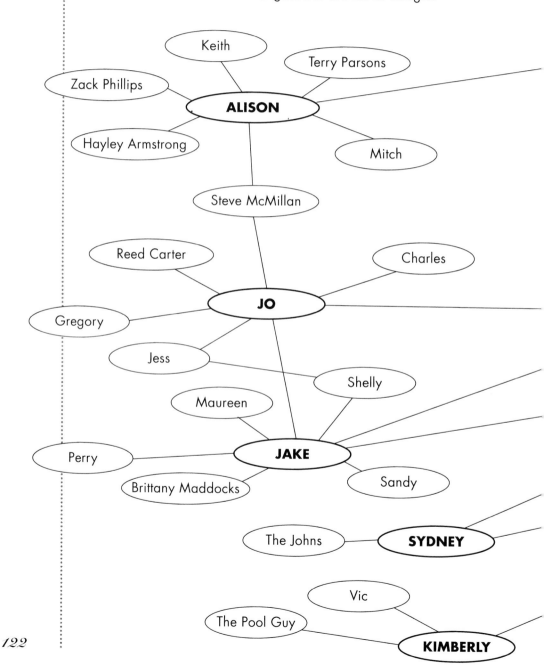

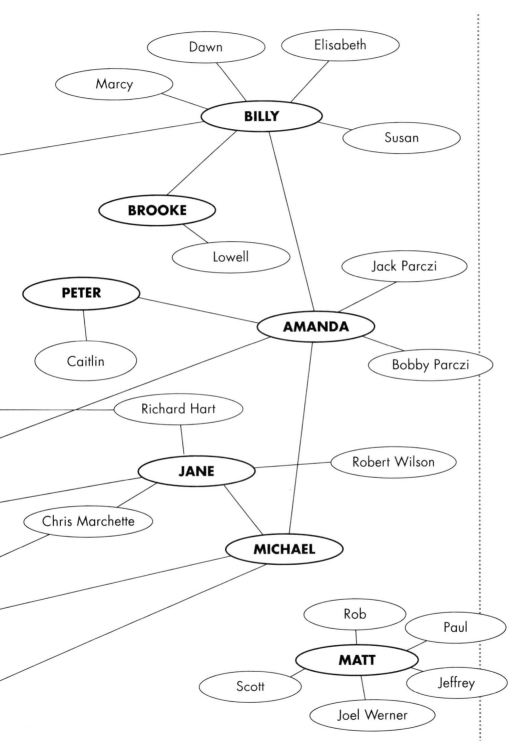

Blondes and Bombshells

THE BIG SHE-BANG

After a long summer's wait, fans finally witnessed Kimberly's wrath unleashed upon the *Melrose* complex, and what a blast it was. Bodies flew and fluttered slo-mo to the smoky ground. An immediate chorus of oh-my-gods filled the air like a Gregorian chant as the dust settled. Soon the Wilshire Hospital emergency room was jammed with the victims of Shaw's madness. The only corpse was Mackenzie Hart—everyone else got away with bruises and mussed hair (well, except for Alison—but keep reading).

And wither the evil lady doctor herself? Well, given the gaggle of witnesses who watched her gleefully detonate the bombs, this was one scheme she couldn't pawn off on Jane or Sydney with a cheap wig and neat alibi. A shaky Kimberly huddled in psychiatric lockup, not remembering her own involvement in the maelstrom. Peter Burns, who had gallantly fished her out of the pool, hovered at her side. Bits and pieces of what she had done flitted across her brain, but Kimberly simply couldn't comprehend how or why she would have bombed Amanda's real estate tax shelter off the map.

Try as he might, Peter could not convince Kimberly that pleading insanity would be her best bet—or at least, a step up from prison without possibility of parole. Michael and Sydney's presence at the courtroom hearing was enough to make "Henry" reappear and give Kimberly that nudge over the edge that convinced the judge she was, indeed, crackers. Her high-flying dive across the courtroom toward the conniving duo was a feat worthy of the Flying Wallendas.

Back in her padded cell, Kimberly descended deeper into hysteria when Michael and Sydney popped in to rub their newfound passion in her face. Not even the zap of electroshock she'd had could keep her from screaming at them to stop hounding her.

Of course, Michael got in a dig at Sydney, too. The redheaded vixen was ecstatic to be back in Dr. Mancini's loving arms. But once they'd

Roll out the red carpet: Shue and Locklear at the forty-fifth Emmy Awards.

driven Kimberly up the wall, Mikey dumped her like a hot potato. "Thanks for fooling my looney tunes wife, Syd. Now beat it," he jeered. At least Sydney's hurt healed fast enough for her to agree to answer the phones at the newly-minted Burns-Mancini medical offices.

HOW DID HENRY'S GARDEN GROW?

Peter managed to lasso Kimberly's mother Marion into coming in from Ohio to help him crack her daughter's case. After much hand-wringing and eye-rolling, Mama finally 'fessed up that there was, indeed, a heinous Henry in her little girl's past—the family's gardener. He'd tried to plant a bit of his seed in Mrs. Shaw and Kimberly found him mid-attack. Seizing a knife, she killed her mother's assailant, but was forever after plagued by his vile image. Marion was content to leave the matter undisturbed, so Kimberly's internal demon was her own lonely, mysterious secret.

Armed with an explanation for his patient's madness, Peter secured a release for the newly-shrunk Shaw. Off she trotted to his house, with only a pesky wrist monitor between her and freedom. Michael and Sydney's fevered imaginations ran overtime cooking up a scheme to hire an actor to literally dog Dr. Shaw's footsteps and kick her back over the edge.

In no time, Kimberly was spotting her deranged alter ego in the *Melrose* laundry room and outside the windows of Peter's house. But the broad didn't scare that easily—she summoned all her nerve, whacked him with a baseball bat (Jake would have approved) and tackled the terrified thespian, ripping off his fake mustache. Deliriously free at last, Kimberly bestowed a lovely thank-you bouquet on a befuddled Michael and Sydney.

Kimberly's pithy comments to talk radio host Dr. Joyce Brothers netted her a new career on the air, and life began to look up. The unbelievable—even for *Melrose*—happened when the Bombing Babe moved into the very apartment complex she'd blown up months earlier. If she could only persuade Peter she was a more suitable object for his affections than that pesky little blonde Amanda. . .

I'M YOUR BIGGEST FAN

Kimberly's sultry radio performance brought out the beast in one devoted listener, Vic. Turned out he was the same dude who picked her up at Shooters *and* tuned in faithfully to taunt her on air. When Kimberly unwittingly scurried back to his place for some passionate playtime, she soon found herself bound and gagged, with a knife at her throat. Never underestimate this woman—a few karate kicks later, Kimberly was back in charge and sent the scurvy rat on his way.

Convinced her many trials and tribulations could be put to good use, Dr. Shaw returned to Wilshire Memorial as a psychiatric resident. With her brains and, ah, *unusual* life experiences, she was sure she'd make the perfect therapist. And who better to lay down on her couch than lovesick Sydney? That's right, the current Mrs. Mancini was busily assisting ex-Mrs. M. Number Two in her scheme to recapture Michael's heart—or parts south, at least.

LOVE IS BLIND

While most of the complex residents escaped with tastefully placed scratches and bruises, Alison emerged from the explosion blind. As she simultaneously insisted to Billy that he back off *and* arranged for him to rebutton her shirt or catch her naked after a shower, Alison kept the befuddled bridegroom as distracted as possible. Wifey Brooke spit nails.

A guilt-ridden Amanda agreed to rehire Alison at D&D, and assigned Brooke to help Alison navigate her dark new world. Within weeks, Alison's sight was restored, but she kept that nugget of knowledge to herself as long as she could.

Hayley, as anxious as Alison to bust up the newlyweds, approached her with a ruse that they pretend to be in love to upset both Billy and Brooke. After much rolling of eyes, Alison gave it a go. Their farce soon became the real thing, much to their mutual surprise.

Brooke was aghast at the thought of Alison living in luxury in her Daddy's home; Billy begged her to let it go. True love's course wasn't all smooth, though. Hayley's mood swings and locked rooms caused Alison to repack those suitcases. (She oughta get luggage with wheels.) After Alison and Billy were almost eighty-sixed in a plane crash, she and Hayley tied the knot in a hastily arranged Mexican wedding ceremony.

Hayley's business ventures began to cave in on him, and poor Alison was left in the dark. Though she longed to be a genuine partner, her husband pulled away. So far away that he fell overboard from the yacht and turned up dead. Alison learned at the reading of his will that he'd divorced her in secret.

OH, BROTHER . . .

Jake managed to escape the bombing by taking a flying leap off a high rise, mid-battle with Jess. Jess ended up dead in a jangled heap. Jo desperately tried to console Jake in his bitter mourning, but he pushed her away. Instead, he hosted a drunken celebration at Shooters. By evening's end, even Jake knew there was nothing to cheer about as

On the Nightstand

What clutters the bedside tables of our favorite *Melrose* guys and dolls? We got the following reports from their cleaning ladies, but, hey, you didn't hear that from us.

Kimberly: Johnnie Cochran's phone number
Earplugs
New England Journal of Medicine
Freud's *Interpretation of Dreams*

Michael: Condoms
Nail clippers
Remote control
Penthouse

Jake: Public Defender's phone number
Ace Bandage (for bruised knuckles)
Can of Budweiser
Road & Track
30 Days to a Better Vocabulary

Jo: Gun
Flashlight
War and Peace
Vanity Fair

Matt: *Howl* by Allen Ginsberg
Box of Kleenex

Billy: Harmonica
Mad magazine
All I Really Need to Know I Learned in Kindergarten
Norman Mailer's *Oswald's Tale: An American Mystery*

Brooke: Chanel night cream

Life preserver

Electra from *Collected Greek Tragedies*

Town & Country

Alison: Sleep mask

Cold compresses

Dental floss

Advertising Age

Backlash by Susan Faludi

Jane: Sketch pad & pencil

Women's Wear Daily

Vogue

Obsession: The Lives and Times of Calvin Klein

Sydney: Gum

Nail polish remover

People

Soap Opera Digest

Jackie Collins's *Hollywood Wives*

The Bible

Amanda: Cartier watch

Borghese hand cream

Wall Street Journal

How to Argue and Win Every Time by Gerry Spence

Damage by Josephine Hart

Richard: Rolex watch

GQ

Urn for Mackenzie's ashes

Sleep mask

Peter: *Golf Digest*

Phone numbers of maid service and pool cleaners

Michael Crichton's *Coma*

he unburdened his heart to Jo. They resolved to rebuild their tattered relationship.

Just as they set their sights on romantic happiness then more remnants of Jess's soggy life cluttered up the scene. Seemed he'd left behind an ex-wife, Shelly, who innocently—hah—turned up on Jake's doorstep looking for her estranged husband. Never one to turn away a lady needing a bed (remember Brittany Maddocks?), Jake soon had a shapely roomie. Jo sighed and renewed her subscription to *Migraine Monthly*.

Shelly quickly moved from houseguest, complete with an array of teeny-weenie bikinis, to bookkeeper at Shooters. While Jake clomped around in his chunky workboots, the little miss wrangled him into buying a new computer system and inaugurating periodic Dance Nights to beef up business. All the while, she pouted and primped, attempting to lure him. It looked like all her exertions were useless—until Jo mentioned a business trip to Hawaii with Richard Hart. A sure-he'd-been-duped Jake finally gave in and plastered himself all over Shelly atop the back office desk. Jo walked in on them, promptly turned on her heel, and jetted off to Hawaii just to prove Jake right.

No sooner was Jake enjoying himself with Shelly than Matt, his part-time waiter, spoiled the party. Seemed Shelly had more than lovin' on her mind: She was busy tinkering with the barkeep's books. Stubborn as ever, Jake refused to believe Matt's warning until the damaging bank statements were staring him in the face. When he raced to Shelly's apartment to confront her, the lady flipped out as she watched her nifty embezzlement scheme slip through her greedy fingers. And her hysterics sure weren't pretty—luckily, the knife she waved around didn't make a scratch on Jake's lovely face, and she was arrested.

BUSINESS BEFORE PLEASURE

Jane survived the blast, but it seemed her sensibilities got jostled by the jolt. "Success at any price" was her new mantra, starting with her callous suggestion that Richard bury his dead wife Mackenzie under her maiden name in order not to ruffle customer feathers. Richard was appalled by her bloodless ambition, but he went along. He *was* smitten, after all.

Jane's aggressive moves escalated. The topper came when she grabbed the mike at the fashion show and chattered to the assembled fashion press that she, and not Mackenzie Hart, was the designer of the whole line. Distracted by Jane's ample charms, Richard continued to overlook her octopussy maneuvers. At Richard's urging, Jo nudged Jane into accepting his marriage proposal. Soon the (temporarily) happy fella had bestowed a nice chunk of ice on the third finger, left hand of his determined damsel.

Jo couldn't shake that nagging feeling after Jane confided that she didn't really love Richard. Oh, she liked him, all right, and he had fabulous connections for business, and she'd learn to love him and . . . Jo just kept thinking the whole mess wasn't kosher. By the time Richard and Jane threw a posh engagement party, a tipsy Jo's champagned-induced candor let Richard know Jane's loving wasn't on the level.

Soon the coupling was kaput, though business was booming. Jane kept that rock firmly on her finger, determined she could sway Richard's heart. Her proposed "working vacation" to Hawaii turned from paradise to nightmare when Richard invited Jo along, then arranged for Jane to be conveniently dragged back to New York.

Richard found loving Jo much more to his liking. An enraged Jane socked her former friend right in the kisser, and the atmosphere at Hart-Mancini Designs simmered just below the boiling point. The winning partnership teetered at the brink of extinction.

OUT OF MY WAY, SISTER

Jane decided to pretend to seduce Michael to arouse Richard's jealousy. Unfortunately, she missed her target and aroused Sydney's envy instead. Hoping to get Jane out of Michael's system, little sis slipped some potent phenobarbitol (prescription courtesy of Dr. Shaw) into Jane's champagne at the swinging Wilshire Hospital Benefit. Soon Jane revved into overdrive and attacked Michael in a fit of sexual heat that went poof as she suffered a stroke.

A despondent Jane found herself wheelchair-bound and recovering at Casa Mancini. When Michael slipped into her bed for some comfort and joy, she cracked a vase over his head and blurted out her true feelings for the scumbucket. Tail between his legs, he bunked over at Peter's until his beach house was sister-free.

Determined to get Michael back in her arms, Sydney tried to plant Jane at a senior citizen's nursing home. When that flopped, she parked her sister's wheelchair on the beach and romanced Michael for the evening. Only gallant Jake's surprise appearance saved Jane from sleeping with the fishes. The tide had rolled in and was about to carry her off when he carried her ashore and they locked in a passionate embrace. Love pops up in the strangest places. . . .

Matt's life blew up in his face, but this one wasn't Kimberly's fault. Paul Graham did a fine job fingering his clueless paramour for the death of his wife Carolyn. True to trusting form, Matt waltzed into every trap the wily doctor had set up.

Fielding's parents supplied a top-notch criminal attorney, but Matt refused her services when he feared his folks' only motivation was to keep the muddle quiet so there'd be no discussion of his homosexuality in the trial coverage. Once he recovered from his tirade, Matt saw a different side to the story when his parents put up their home as collateral for his bail.

Whirling like a dervish, Matt set out to disrupt every legal maneuver his lawyer, Alycia Barnett, carefully arranged. First, he confronted Paul—with his fists, no less—in plain sight at the hospital, fueling police theories that they had acted in cahoots. Then he concocted a fake letter from Carolyn that implicated Paul, and wired himself to entrap the doc. At the showdown, Paul pulled a gun, but he ended up being the one shot when the thing went off. Fortunately, the cops and Matt's lawyer arrived in time to hear Paul's confession as he gasped his last breaths.

But more rotten luck awaited. Homophobe and hospital bigwig Dr. Hobbs ruined a perfectly good welcome-back party when he fired Matt during the festivities. Matt dithered about whether to pursue *another* sex discrimination lawsuit, but Michael's ever persuasive arguments won the day. Can you say "deposition"? Matt could, and did, and Hobbs was eventually fired.

The whole pickle made Matt more reflective than usual, and after some heart-to-hearts with Dad just prior to the old man's fatal heart attack, Matt decided to return to medical school. In another classic Matt and Michael pas de deux, Michael first berated him for even thinking he had the cojones to make it as a medicine man; then turned gung-ho and fixed Matt's failing test score on the hospital computer so his buddy would be admitted.

At the Shooters celebration for his success on the reentry exam, a beaming Michael showed Matt how he'd altered the test scores as payback for Matt's help with those nasty blood alcohol levels after his drunken car accident. The two men exchanged a long look.

Matt took another stab at love when he met Alan, an emergency room patient. Soon the doctor in training and his aspiring actor boyfriend were enjoying moonlit nights and sunny days. When Alan decided to move to

Manhattan and make a name for himself on stage, an ever-supportive Matt drove him to the airport for a big sendoff. Throwing caution to the wind, Matt declared his love and urged Alan to move in with him instead of winging off to the Big Apple.

Alan landed a one-day stint as a doctor on a soap and Matt promised to stop studying long enough to offer a few medical pointers. That is, he promised after Alan pouted and complained that Matt never had time for him.

BABBLING BROOKE

You gotta feel some sympathy for Brooke. She'd no sooner changed out of her backless satin wedding gown than she nearly got blown sky-high while stopping off at Billy's to grab the tickets for their honeymoon getaway. Next thing she knew, her hunky new husband was sending boffo bouquets to his old girlfriend and lingering at her side.

So, Brooke got a tad jealous. She threatened Alison, sweeping a heap of dishes off her countertop for good measure. And, oops, Brooke also forgot to mention to her hubby that she wasn't bothering with that pesky diaphragm. She got pregnant and convinced Billy it was good news. Well, married couples do have babies, don't they? Maybe she went *too* far when she cut her father out of her baby's life, but Brooke is Brooke.

For all her wailing, though, Brooke did side with Billy when Hayley delivered his umpteenth ultimatum. She lugged her suitcase over to Melrose Place and settled in. (Right, as if all her duds fit into one jumbo tote.)

With no honeymoon in sight, Brooke busied herself in other ways. Furious that Amanda had demoted her in favor of Little Miss Sightless, Brooke wreaked havoc when she hunted around in Amanda's locked personal files. (Is it just us, or does it seem incredible that Amanda would keep those incriminating documents in her office? Or that she'd keep the key conveniently taped to the underside of her desk instead of in her safe-deposit box? Oh, well.)

AMANDA'S BAND O' GOLD

Armed with the amazing discovery that Amanda harbored a secret past, complete with a husband, Brooke was off to Miami to see for herself what kind of man Amanda would marry. After a quick research trip at the local library, she was knocking on Jack Parezi's door. The sight of Amanda's portrait hanging eerily in the living room was enough to give her goosebumps. What Brooke didn't know was that Jack was a sadistic wife-beater.

Back in L.A., a terrified Ms. Woodward—or is that Mrs. Parezi?—gave Brooke the swanky corner office and fancy vice presidency, no questions asked. She even demoted Alison to sweeten the deal.

For her largesse, Amanda got nothing but headaches. Jack tracked Brooke down straightaway, and followed her trail of bread crumbs straight to the office door of his not-so-dead wife. Claiming he needed a divorce so he could marry fiancée Rita, Jack instead insinuated himself into Amanda's life with gusto. Terrified that his abusive habits would resurface and signal her doom, she entrusted Billy with a key to her safe-deposit box, and showed him harrowing pictures of her battered body.

Brooke continued to ignore the threat Jack posed. First, she blabbed about Amanda's party to celebrate the rebuilding of the apartments, so Jack showed up and dogged his spouse's every step. Next, Brooke brought him back to D&D as a client—the only one she managed to land besides her own father. Amanda felt his grip tightening, and she knew it was bad news.

JACK SPLAT

Arriving at Jack's palatial L.A. manse to meet his fiancée, Amanda was shocked to see her portrait gracing the living room. What would Rita think? she wondered to Jack. There *is* no Rita, baby, there's only you, Jack leered. The danger of being alone with him sent her into flight; unfortunately, she raced up the stairs, instead of out the door. Jack scampered after her. As they tussled, he tumbled over the banister and crashed into the foyer. A panicked Amanda called Peter, who sized up the danger and personally admitted Jack to the hospital. A suspicious Michael sniffed around, but backed off when Amanda explained her abused past with Jack.

All that remained now was her fervent hope that Jack wouldn't emerge from his coma. In a burst of dread, she stormed Peter's office and swore she'd kill Jack if he awoke and recovered. A wily Sydney, ever ready to stockpile blackmail ammunition, taped the incriminating tirade for future use.

Sure enough, as Jack rallied, he grabbed his beloved wife by the throat. Amanda punched him in the jaw—and all while Sydney lurked in the doorway. Jack finally flatlined. Drs. Burns and Mancini hustled the autopsy along to hold off Parezi's legal eagles.

Sydney assembled Amanda, Peter, and Michael to lay out the terms of her keeping her lips zipped—half of Amanda's stake in Jack's estate, thank you very much. Peter and Amanda pulled the rug out from under

Syd's blackmail scheme by reducing Amanda's inheritance share to one dollar in exchange for the sealing of the incriminating autopsy results. Ooh, fifty cents to the lady with the lovely red hair.

THE APPLE DOESN'T FALL FAR FROM THE TREE

Left heartbroken and confused, Alison buried herself in work and tried to be a good friend to Billy *and* Brooke. However crazed Brooke became, Alison felt an obligation to Hayley's memory to take the high road.

Meanwhile, Brooke was getting lowdown and dirty. She'd clearly inherited Daddy's manic highs and morose lows, if not his money. Determined to grab the millions left in trust to her unborn baby, she persisted in telling Billy she'd miscarried, even after her OB informed her she'd never been pregnant. That little cat was soon out of the bag, and Billy, angry at being duped once more, threatened divorce and rushed to Alison's comforting arms.

Good girl Ali marched him right back to Brooke, who had slit her wrists in the meantime. A guilty Billy tried to stand by his wife's side, but when she first trashed Alison's apartment and left nasty slogans on the walls and next redecorated Billy's kitchen with spaghetti sauce and broken dinnerware, his compassion bottomed out. Their nasty divorce was halted by a drunken Brooke drowning in the complex pool.

DO I ICE HER OR DO I MARRY HER?

Amanda's relief at Jack's death was but a moment's quiet on her roller coaster of love. No sooner was Peter blissfully back in her arms than Jack's brother Bobby bopped into town. And it wasn't just a social call—The Family had dispatched little bro to kill Amanda as revenge for Jack's untimely demise.

Just one little problem. Bobby and Amanda were each other's first love. At the sight of her divine form and adorable face, Bobby fell again, hard. He craftily manipulated Peter out of the picture by making a generous donation to the hospital, for which Peter got the credit, and having the family attorney, Alycia, settle a pesky malpractice action for the less-than-grateful doc.

Peter's efforts to get rid of the big lug and keep Amanda to himself were a tad heavy-handed, and the ever-independent Ms. Woodward told the good doctor to take a hike. Meanwhile, she hotfooted over to Bobby and smooched it up.

And to find out how Amanda and the rest of the gang fare, you have to stay tuned.

Now Playing

We took a quick peek at the rental slips from the local video store. Now we know what the *Melrose* gang checks out when they're up for a movie night at home.

Billy:
Babe
Star Wars
E.T., The Extra-Terrestrial
The Brady Bunch Movie
An Affair to Remember

Amanda:
Disclosure
The Lady Eve
An Affair to Remember

Matt:
Crimson Tide
Philadelphia
An Affair to Remember

Kimberly:
Sybil
Dr. Strangelove or How I Learned to Stop Worrying and Love the Bomb
An Affair to Remember

Alison:
When Harry Met Sally . . .
The Bridges of Madison County
Clean and Sober
An Affair to Remember

Jo:
Losing Isaiah
Manhattan
Blow-up

Sabrina
The Sure Thing
An Affair to Remember

Jake:
Mad Max
Billy Jack
Shane
Rocky
Easy Rider
An Affair to Remember

Sydney:
Breakfast at Tiffany's
Take the Money and Run
Pretty Woman
An Affair to Remember

Michael:
Alfie
The Man Who Loved Women
Shampoo
An Affair to Remember

Jane:
Unzipped
Clueless
Funny Face
An Affair to Remember

Brooke:
Chinatown
Father of the Bride
An Affair to Remember

Kristin Davis

Is it just us, or did Kristin Davis take extraordinary delight in playing Brooke Armstrong at the edge of decency? Her tête-a-têtes with Hayley, her Daddy Dearest, bordered on the incestuous; her gleeful threats to a blinded Alison, complete with a vicious swipe that sent the dishes crashing off the kitchen countertop, were straight out of *What Ever Happened to Baby Jane?*

So where did Davis get the spunky attitude? She credits her ingrained southern lady upbringing in Columbia, South Carolina. "There was a lot of maneuvering around men. It didn't really foster a directness," she confided to *Entertainment Weekly*. But Davis was always up front about her desire to act.

As the dutiful only step-daughter of a professor, she trooped north to Rutgers University in New Jersey. But the siren call of Manhattan was too strong a lure. She moved to the city and waitressed to pay the rent, like countless other ambitious actresses. Davis eventually made the rounds in regional theater and appeared in commercials for Odor Eaters and Kraft Salad Dressing. She nabbed small parts on the daytime dramas *Another World* and *General Hospital*, and even dated one of her *Another World* costars, Matt Crane, who plays Matt Cory.

Her biggest pre-*Melrose* break was a steamy turn during NBC's 1994 smash freshman season of *ER*. Her clothes-on seduction of George Clooney (as Doug Ross) raised temperatures across America, to the red-faced astonishment of her parents. While turns on *The Larry Sanders Show*, *Dr. Quinn, Medicine Woman*, and in the feature *Nine Months* (with Hugh Grant) were tamer, Davis admits that she primed her folks before they tuned in to see her as debutante Brooke on *Melrose*. "I had to go through a whole thing with them about the show's sexual content. They thought *ER* was a little upsetting—and I was fully clothed in that!" she related to *Entertainment Weekly*.

Davis's parents should heave a sigh of relief that their daughter didn't get the part she originally tried out for—trigger-happy Kimberly. As for Davis herself, she found life on planet *Melrose* just ducky, right up to her watery demise—the signature sayonara of the Armstrong clan.

Know Your "Melrose" Trivia

For answers, see page 154.

SEASON ONE

1. What is the street address of the *Melrose Place* apartment complex?
2. What is the name of the roommate who moved out on Alison in the very first episode, sticking her with the entire month's rent?
3. Who was Alison's first male boss at D&D?
4. When Kelly Taylor pined away for Jake in the early episodes of season one, what other *90210* characters hung around the Melrose Avenue area with her?
5. Before Billy started driving a cab to support himself, what work was he training himself to do?
6. Rhonda was all excited about dating Daniel, but he was after something besides romance. What was it?
7. What product was D&D promoting at a swanky reception that Alison attended with her boss at the time?
8. Who was the original owner of Shooters?
9. While driving his cab, Billy met and had a brief fling with a flirty female fare. What was her name?
10. What famous doctor appeared in a dream of Billy's and gave him advice about his love life?
11. What was it that Alison was afraid to tell Billy about his first screenplay?
12. Perry, an ex-girlfriend of Jake's, wanted him to take part in a phony art scam. She also had an addictive habit—to what?
13. At the party when Alison was chosen as the Advertising Account Executive of the Year, which game show host made a cameo appearance?
14. Rick, a mail room worker at D&D, stole Alison's idea for a campaign for his father's account. What was the product involved?
15. Which original character had an abortion at sixteen?
16. What was the name of the neighborhood paper for which Billy wrote a column?
17. What are the names of Billy's father and mother?

18. In what business was Billy's dad?
19. What was the name of Rhonda's friend who danced in a professional troupe?
20. Why did Jake seek Alison's assistance on the sly in season one?
21. Where were Alison and Jake when they shared a romantic kiss?
22. Who is Dr. Aviva Lester?
23. What was Alison's pet name for her car?
24. Why was Alison emotionally attached to her car?
25. In what line of work was Sandy's boyfriend Paul?
26. What was the name of the comedienne girlfriend Billy picked up in his cab?
27. What caused Billy's romance with her to fizzle?
28. What was the name of Jake's mother?
29. Who played Jake's mother?
30. How much is the rent on one of the *MP* apartments?
31. Where did Alison meet Keith?
32. What kind of organization did Keith run?
33. Why couldn't Billy qualify for a credit card?
34. What's Matt's profession?
35. What was Matt's first job when the show began?
36. What was the name of Keith's wife?
37. Why did Sarah Goldstein, Matt's lawyer in the sex discrimination lawsuit against the Teen Youth Center, waive her fees?
38. Who was the roommate who moved in with Rhonda after Sandy left for New York City?
39. What actress played that part?
40. Why did Sandy move to New York?
41. Where did Matt work after he was fired from the Teen Youth Center?
42. What were the names of Matt's parents?
43. Why did Rhonda ask her new roommate to move out?
44. Why did Alison feel particularly guilty about her affair with Keith, who was married?

Josie Bissett

IT'S ALL ROSY FOR JOSIE

Josie Bissett is a study in contradictions. While most models are at least five foot ten, runway vet Bissett is only five foot five. One of the younger members of the *Melrose* cast, (she's just twenty-six), Bissett's settled down in a dizzily happy marriage to ex *Silk Stalkings'* star Rob Estes. She effortlessly carries off the "designer" look of her character, Jane Mancini, yet in real life, she's a tomboy. Devoted to her brood of six brothers and sisters (three of whom are adopted), she left home at sixteen and made her way in the world. Pretty intriguing complexities for the woman who was kept in sweetness mode the longest on *Melrose Place*.

Unlike brain-drain Jane, Bissett has shown drive and determination since her childhood in Seattle. While her parents ran a glass company, Bissett kicked along for twelve years on soccer teams while also squeezing in track, basketball and softball. Away from sports, she used her striking good looks to launch a modeling career. She knew that because she was vertically challenged (for a model, that is), she was better off trying her luck somewhere other than America—so she packed her passport and winged off to Japan. Her exotic, blonde silhouette fit the bill for the Far East audience.

Tokyo offered Bissett limited opportunities for anything other than modeling, so she moved to L.A. in 1988 to cast her rod and reel into the acting pond. Her first forays before the camera came in Italian quickie films like *Desire* and *The Hitcher in the Dark*. After a two-shot guest appearance on *The Hogan Family*, Bissett joined the cast as Mark's (Jeremy Licht) girlfriend Cara during the show's final season. *Doogie Howser, M.D.*, *Parker Lewis*, and *Quantum Leap* continued to help pay the bills, as well as a television movie, *A Family for Joe*, which starred Robert Mitchum.

One of Bissett's most well-known spots was not in a television show, but in a commercial. That was Bissett ambling and rambling in the famous black-and-white ad for Calvin Klein's Obsession perfume. Directed by David Lynch, the minimovie spots were the talk of the TV industry when they first aired.

In 1991 Bissett hit pay dirt in Oliver Stone's *The Doors*. Re-creating the trippy aura of the drug and booze-soaked world of rocker Jim Morrison (played by Val Kilmer), *The Doors* was one of the most authentic dramatizations of the tumult of the 1960s. Originally hired as a "groupie," Bissett snagged the role of Lynn Krieger, wife of guitarist Robbie, when Krieger himself visited the set and was struck by Bissett's resemblance to his old lady.

Although Jane Mancini's made Bissett famous, at the end of last season, the actress demanded some changes in her character—and the writers heard her. "In a sense, Jane hasn't had a chance—*I* haven't had a chance as an actress to show what I can do on this show," she told *TV Guide*. As the fourth season has unfolded, Jane's a wallflower no more.

Jane Mancini rose from the ashes of the bombed apartment complex like a phoenix. With Mackenzie Hart dead, she boldly stepped up her control of the dead woman's design firm while brazenly wooing confused widower Richard. Who would've imagined prim little Jane showing up in his office in a trench coat, whipping it off to reveal little more than a come hither smile? "It's. . . great. Jane will do anything to take over the company. She'll manipulate people, she'll be bad, she'll do whatever it takes. She gets to be a mini-Heather," Josie gloated to *Entertainment Weekly*.

Bissett's quest to expand her image continued with her latest made-for-television movie role in ABC's *Dare to Love*. She played a vulnerable and confused schizophrenic who escapes into the world of stripping and pole dancing. And on Conan O'Brien's *Late Night*, she merrily showed off a tattoo inked dangerously high on her leg. Make no mistake; Josie's no shrinking violet. The lady's a hothouse gardenia in full bloom.

45. Which *Melrose* hunk tried to put the moves on Jo first?
46. Why was Jake suspicious about the expensive bracelet Jo asked him to pawn for her?
47. What was the name of the demanding boss who bought out the dress shop where Jane worked?
48. Why did Jo move to L.A. from New York City?
49. What surprise did Jake's ex-girlfriend Colleen have in store for him?
50. Why did Alison need surgery at the end of season one?
51. How did Alison pay for the surgery without medical insurance?
52. Where did Terrence want to take Rhonda for the Christmas holidays?
53. What kind of business did Terrence own?
54. Where did Rhonda's parents live?
55. What did Sydney do before she came to visit Jane in L.A.?
56. What did Alison do as Billy's date at the Advertising Association Ball?
57. What was Jo's husband's name?
58. What "special dish" did Jake cook for Jo?
59. What problem did Amanda have with the photos Jo took of Rex Weldon, the tennis superstar who was featured in a D&D underwear campaign?
60. What game did Amanda, Alison, and Billy play up at Amanda's parents' lake house?
61. What game did Jane and Michael play with his supervisor Dr. Levin and his wife Erica?
62. What did Jo do with her $50,000 divorce settlement?
63. Whom did Terrence hire to decorate the dream house he bought for Rhonda?
64. What dangerous item did Jo keep in her apartment?
65. Who was the old friend of Jane and Michael who briefly dated Jane after Michael left her for Kimberly?
66. What actor played that role?
67. How did Billy's father die?
68. What was the name of Billy's sister?
69. Where did she live?
70. Why did Jake's ex-girlfriend Perry call him in a panic?
71. Billy filled his resume with lies to land the job at *Escapade* magazine. From what college did he claim he graduated?
72. What was the name of Billy's boss at *Escapade?*
73. How did Jo's mother die?

74. What was the name of Lucy's fiancé?

75. Where were Billy and Alison the first time they had sex?

76. At the end of season one, what news did Amanda tell Billy that almost put the kibosh on his new romance with Alison?

77. What bizarre floral gift did Keith have delivered to Alison at work?

78. What did Keith use to whack Billy over the head with when he attacked him?

SEASON TWO

1. When Jo and Jake decided to move in together at the beginning of season two, whose apartment was used and why?

2. How did Keith injure himself to make it look like the same person who had attacked him had also gone after Billy?

3. What was Jake washing in the bathtub at their apartment that made her unhappy?

4. When Jane sued for Michael's future earnings during their divorce, he whined and pleaded that she drop the suit. Jane became so frustrated that she threw some household items at him. What were they?

5. What was the name of Jane's divorce attorney?

6. When Keith attacked Alison, showing his true obsessive colors, how did she fight him off to escape from his hotel room?

7. What strange sight did Billy find when he broke into Keith's Seattle home?

8. What household chore did an eager Sydney do for Michael while his divorce from Jane was pending?

9. For what product did Amanda want Jake to be the ad model?

10. What was the last news we heard about Keith, Alison's stalker?

11. If Matt's gay, why did he marry Katya?

12. What happened to "Jake's Bikes"?

13. What was the name of the wealthy hotel chain owner whom Billy interviewed for *Escapade* magazine?

14. What was the name of his sexy young daughter?

15. When Jane encountered Michael at the supermarket after he'd lied on the stand about his affair with Kimberly, what did she do to him?

16. What was Katya's daughter's name?

17. Who played her?

18. In what business was Steve McMillan, a D&D client?

19. Who played the part of Steve McMillan?

20. Where was Matt and Katya's wedding party?

Out of the Closet

On *Melrose*, women don't just dress—they preen, they primp, and oh, do they strut. Female fans drool with envy; men give thanks to the god of tight skirts.

PASTEL POWER: AMANDA WOODWARD

Those suits are snug as the skin on a grape and small as a eunuch's prospects. And God help Amanda if she has to bend over to pick up a paper clip. But those with their eyes open can tell that Amanda's corporate look requires a "no cleavage" policy at all times. No fussy patterns or prints for this executrix—she's all bold solids, telegraphing her commitment to staying on top.

ACCESSORIZE: KIMBERLY SHAW

Under that austere white lab coat lurks a Satin Doll. Kimberly's seldom caught without her plunging necklines, sexy bras and panties, or shimmering pegnoirs. Being locked up on the psychiatric ward in a—gasp—cotton wraparound put a considerable crimp in her usually sleek style, although that black security wrist band screamed Paloma Picasso.

THE WRINKLED LOOK: ALISON PARKER

She needs a course in Professional Wardrobe 101. Her rumpled outfits look like they've been washed but not ironed. Although when it comes to slouching around in a pair of jeans to whine at Billy, Alison's the Gap girl come to life.

NO WHITE SHOES AFTER LABOR DAY: BROOKE ARMSTRONG

Brooke's sleeveless, collarless dresses reminded us of Donna Reed crossed with a touch of Madonna. Under that plummeting backless wedding gown in which she snagged Billy, we're convinced she wore nothing but Chanel No. 5. Soft pastels belied her saucy maneuvers until the end, when she adopted the "wet look."

PLAIN NO MORE: JANE MANCINI

Now that she's burst out of her kvetchy victim mode, Jane's clothes have shifted from those cloying, billowy granny dresses to tight, short, black-and-white stunners. Happy as a cat that sees cream, she has a brazen look that trumpets "Don't mess with me, fellas."

MOD MANIA: SYDNEY ANDREWS

Sydney's look is as hard to pin down as the tail on the donkey. Low on funds, weak on taste, bewildered by her own ever shifting self-image, Sydney herself never knows what ragtag mix she'll throw on next. Her latest look, a salute to the sixties, complete with teased bouffant and thick eyeliner, however, is a tangerine dream that would make Twiggy proud.

PAINT IT BLACK: JO REYNOLDS

After three seasons in inky ensembles to remind us that she's a New Yorker, Jo has crawled up the color spectrum to dark brown. Women everywhere with thick ankles appreciate her loyalty to leg coverings of all types. Maybe by the time show celebrates its five-hundredth episode, we'll catch her in off-white. Go girl!

21. What was the name of the auto reproduction company Palmer Woodward hired Jake to work for?

22. Matt found out being married put a crimp in his getting dates with guys. Where did he meet Joel, one of his few dates during his marriage to Katya?

23. How did Jane get Michael to stay away from her after their divorce?

24. Why was Billy annoyed by coworker Celia Morales at *Escapade*?

25. What painful confession did Amanda make to Jake about her mother Hillary?

26. What was the name of the madam who ran Syd's escort service?

27. What actress played the madam?

28. On what daytime soap opera did she appear prior to and since *Melrose Place*?

29. What was the name of the movie producer who was Sydney's first John?

30. Who played the role of the producer?

31. What did Michael force Matt to do after the car crash involving him and Kimberly?

32. What upsetting information did Billy find when he read Alison's e-mail at her office?

33. What led Jake to stop covering for Palmer Woodward's fake auto reproduction scheme?

34. Where did Kimberly's mother take her when she was still in a coma after the accident with Michael?

35. What illegal substance did Lauren force on Sydney to keep her in the escort service business?

36. Where did Steve McMillan go to when he left L.A.?

37. What was the name of the no-nonsense nurse Jane hired to take care of Michael at her apartment while she was away for the Christmas holidays?

38. Where was Sydney when she unburdened her heart and quit the hooker game?

39. What pinnacle of adolescent popularity did Alison achieve?

40. Whom did Jo meet at her high school reunion?

41. Who played the old flame?

42. Where did Amanda go to get away from the F.B.I. when they were trying to find her father after he jumped bail?

43. Why did Celia Morales move in with Billy and Alison?

44. Who bailed out Sydney when she was brought in on prostitution charges?

45. What secret was Jeffrey keeping from Matt?
46. What was the problem with the junior editor position Billy got at *Escapade*?
47. What info did Michael blab when Sydney found him passed out from painkillers at his beach house? (Here's a hint: she used it to blackmail him into marrying her.)
48. Who played Sydney and Jane's mother?
49. What did Reed do to Jo after he realized she had discovered the secret storage compartment on the boat was filled with illegal drugs?
50. At Billy and Alison's engagement party, Billy asked Jake to be his best man. But then Jake learned something about Billy that really pissed him off. What was it?
51. What did Jane do when she saw Sydney in the family heirloom wedding gown Sydney intended to wear when she married Michael?
52. What was Reed's unexpected legacy to Jo?
53. What announcement of Alison's stunned Billy after they got engaged?
54. How much money did Jane's grandmother leave to her?
55. Why did Michael get a share of Jane's inheritance from her grandmother?
56. What did Alison do with the old doll Billy found in the basement of her parents' home?
57. What was the name of the handy man who turned out to be a Peeping Tom?
58. Who was the psychiatrist Alison consulted about her persistent nightmares?
59. How did Michael get the chief residency job?
60. How is Hillary Michaels related to Amanda?
61. What's the name of Hillary's business?
62. Why was Kimberly wearing a wig when she returned to the beach house alive?
63. Who was Sarah Owens?
64. What did Hank, Sarah's boyfriend from Iowa, do to Jo?
65. Who was Chas Russell?
66. What was Sydney's stage name as a stripper?
67. How did Kimberly cause Michael to lose the chief resident position?
68. Who was Chris Marchette?
69. What was Alison's sister's name?
70. Who played the role?

Laura Leighton

Laura Leighton sweated through five auditions before Aaron Spelling told his producers she was the girl to grab for the part of Sydney Andrews. And the original gig was for two quick episodes with Syd bopping into town to visit older sis Jane Mancini.

But something radiated from Leighton when she loped onto the screen as Sydney, the poster child for sibling rivalry. Her two-time appearance blossomed into a full-time part as one of the wildest, strangest vixens on prime time. Leighton has managed to do the almost-impossible—infuse her character with evil tempered by innocence. Who else but Sydney would be shocked to discover prostitution exists, then snap to it and become a high-priced hooker? She blackmailed her ex-brother-in-law into matrimony, and promptly stuffed his beach house with smarmy romantic tchotchkes celebrating their "love." Nasty Chris kidnapped her to Las Vegas, but our gal made the most of it, enjoying all the room service perks she could order up.

This whimsical naiveté saves Sydney from being a one-note cliché. Leighton explains her character's motivation as a wacky attempt to measure up to her "perfect" older sister. "Everybody has the potential to be bitchy, you know. The way I see it, Syd's not *bad*. She has her reasons, too. . .But I have to admit that right now, I'm just lucky that I have one of those great roles where I get paid well to be *incredibly* obnoxious," Leighton mused to *Rolling Stone*.

Being obnoxious is obviously a long way from Leighton's own personality. She grew up as Laura Miller in Iowa City, Iowa, the younger of two children (she has a sister, Lisa). From early on,

Leighton's artistic urges emerged with a passion—she grew up playing classical piano, which she says is still her favorite way to unwind after a day of pandering and slandering on *Melrose Place*.

After a post-high school stint in a squeaky clean traveling song-and-dance revue—the Young Americans—Leighton drove to Los Angeles to see if she had the mettle to make it. She paid her dues with the requisite odd jobs and commercials (Pizza Hut and Dep hair gel), and even worked in an L.A. casting office, where she witnessed an up-close look at the brutal rejection that bombards most wannabes. Soon after, she landed *Melrose Place* and became America's dizziest redhead. The exposure from *Melrose* helped launch Leighton into other projects, including two TV movies: *In the Name of Love: A Texas Tragedy* and *The Other Woman*.

Leighton's understandably protective of her alter ego. As she told *Entertainment Weekly*, "You know in *Bewitched*, when there was always music that played when Tabitha was on screen? It was like this *dee-dee-dee-dee-dee*, this little mischievous music. That's sometimes how I read Sydney in the script. I hear this music playing." Coming from someone whose biggest splurge since hitting it big was buying a piano, that kinda makes sense.

71. Who rescued Michael when Kimberly doped up his beer and left him in the garage at the beach house with his car running?

72. What triggered Alison's memory about her father's abuse?

SEASONS THREE AND FOUR

1. What was the formal charge brought against Jane after Michael was run over?

2. Who operated on Michael when he was brought into the hospital after being run down?

3. What did Kimberly tell the police she was doing during the time Michael was run over?

4. Who posted bail for Jane when she was falsely arrested for hitting Michael with her car?

5. Where is Alison from?

6. Why was Billy fired from *Escapade* magazine?

7. What's the name of Jake's boat?

8. When Michael began to regain his memory, one of his first recollections was an intimate habit he shared with Jane. What was it?

9. Why did Jo give up her son for adoption?

10. Matt confronted Kimberly at the hospital and accused her of wearing a wig to set up Jane to take the fall for hitting Michael with her car. When Kimberly laughed at his suggestion, what did Matt do to prove his accusation?

11. Where did Amanda get the money to buy the apartment complex?

12. What was the name of the D&D assistant who blew off Alison's work in favor of doing Billy's (Alison eventually had her fired)?

13. What's the name of the hospital where all *MP* residents go when they're bombed and bruised?

14. When Jake went to see his father, daddy-o did not want to divulge his son's true identity. Who did he say Jake was?

15. One night, Jo and Alison were at Shooters. Alison picked up a very attractive architect named Mitch. When he stood her up the next day, Alison went to his office and did what to display her anger?

16. Skunky Chris Marchette left Sydney a "gift" in her dresser drawer. What was it?

17. What was the name of the hospital committee from which Kimberly was fired by Peter Burns?

18. When Jake returned to L.A. after seeing his father, he reclaimed his apartment. What little zinger did Amanda throw in when he moved back in?

19. How did Michael and Kimberly end up getting married in Las Vegas?
20. What did Alison's friend Susan do for a living?
21. What was Peter Burns's reason for firing Michael?
22. What is the actual location of the exteriors of the *Melrose Place* apartments?
23. Michael went to Amanda to ask for her help in getting him reinstated at the hospital after Peter fired him. What did he agree to give in return?
24. Alison got involved with a rough-and-tumble guy named Zach. What did he do for a living?
25. Alison was too strung out and hungover to attend Jo's custody hearing. Jo was so pissed off that she made a decision which upset Alison a great deal. What was it?
26. What's Alison's booze of choice?
27. When Alison was arrested for drunk driving after hitting a kid on a bicycle, who bailed her out?
28. Chris Marchette fleeced Jane and Mancini Designs out of a sizable chuck of change. What was the amount?
29. When Chris kidnapped Syd, where did he take her?
30. Where did Bruce Teller hang himself?
31. When Sydney decided she'd had enough of Chris (when he kidnapped her), whom did she call to rescue her?
32. Which city did Sydney live before moving to Los Angeles?
33. After Amanda became president of D&D, Peter showed up at her apartment with an invitation for her to join him in Lake Tahoe. He also brought along what gift as an inducement?
34. Alison met a guy named Terry Parsons when she was in rehab. What did he do for a living?
35. Why did Amanda give Bruce's sister money for Bruce's kids' college tuitions?
36. What weakness did Alison and Caitlin, the efficiency expert, have in common?
37. How did Peter set up Amanda to be fired as president of D&D?
38. Who played Rikki, the woman who got Syd involved in a cult?
39. Where does Alison's sister live?
40. Who told Amanda that she had cancer?
41. When Sydney tried to leave the cult, Martin and his followers found her and punished her. What did they do?
42. Jo's apartment was trashed after she took some incriminating pho-

tos of a cop violently beating someone up. Where were the pictures actually being kept?

43. Where is the set where *Melrose Place* is filmed?

44. Why did Michael and Amanda end up in the same hotel digs in New York?

45. How was Brooke Armstrong first introduced on *Melrose*?

46. What was the name of the campaign that netted Alison the "Outstanding Advertising Executive" award?

47. Where did Jake travel to for his mother's funeral?

48. After a particularly long night of work, what did Billy and Alison do in her office?

49. When Alison was temporarily blind, what trick did she pull to get Billy to see her naked?

50. After marrying Billy, Brooke was expecting to get a fat inheritance from her mother's estate. How much money did she actually receive?

51. On what grounds did Michael threaten to divorce Kimberly?

52. What was the name of Brooke's father?

53. What's the name of Kimberly's mother?

54. Where did Brooke track down Jack Parezi?

55. When Kimberly was plotting her revenge on the *Melrose Place* residents, she kept seeing someone named Henry who encouraged her delusional ravings. In reality, who was Henry?

56. Which *Melrose* cast member was a roommate of *MP* creator Darren Star at U.C.L.A.?

57. Stephen Fanning was the actor originally hired to play Billy Campbell. He was let go before the first episode. But he later worked with Courtney Thorne-Smith (Alison). What was the project?

58. What movie does Billy like to watch on Halloween?

59. What was the name of Jack Parezi's fictional fiancée?

60. There are five mistakes in this book. Can you find them?

Answers

1. 4616 Melrose Place
2. Natalie Miller
3. Hal Barber
4. Donna and David
5. Dance instruction at Arthur Murray's
6. He wanted Rhonda to sell his vitamin line at her aerobics classes.
7. Canyon Ranch Cooler
8. Delia—she also gave career advice to Sandy, who was a Shooter's waitress.
9. Marcy
10. Dr. Ruth Westheimer
11. She thought it stank.
12. Snorting cocaine
13. Chuck Woolery, of *The Love Connection*
14. Sunscreen
15. Sandy
16. The *Melrose Weekly*
17. William and Joan
18. He had a furniture store
19. Theresa
20. He wanted her to help him prepare for his G.E.D. exam
21. Atop Mulholland Drive at night
22. The soap opera neurosurgeon character that Sandy moved to New York to play
23. Betsy
24. She lost her virginity in the backseat.
25. He worked at a nursery.
26. Dawn
27. She had a young son, which was too much responsibility for Billy.
28. Stella
29. Anita Morris, who starred in the Broadway show *Nine*.

30. About $800 per month
31. On Melrose Avenue, of course!
32. An environmental group concerned with protecting the ocean
33. He had defaulted on a student loan he took out for personal expenses while in college.
34. Social worker
35. He worked at a youth center for runaway teens.
36. Lily
37. She felt that the case would generate so much publicity that she'd eventually get more business because of it.
38. Carrie Fellows
39. Rae Dawn Chong
40. She got a part on a soap opera.
41. At a burger joint as a waiter
42. Constance and Matt Sr.
43. Carrie was a neat freak, and ultimately they had a fight over the proper way to clean a frying pan.
44. Her father had cheated on her mother when she was a girl.
45. Billy. He approached her with champagne, but she rebuffed him.
46. It was inscribed "Beth," short for her full name, "Jo Beth."
47. Kay Beacon
48. She hated her empty socialite life and her alcoholic husband.
49. Jake had fathered her son, David.
50. She had a benign tumor that had to be removed.
51. Michael arranged for her to be a teaching patient at the hospital.
52. Aspen
53. He ran a posh restaurant.
54. San José, California
55. She was a college student.
56. She ditched him for Danny, a cute V.P. from D&D accounting.
57. Charles
58. His special pasta with clam sauce.
59. Jo took shots of him bare-bottomed, holding the undies.

60. Truth or Dare
61. Golf
62. She loaned Jake money so he could start up his store, Jake's Bikes.
63. Carrie, her ex-roommate from hell
64. A gun
65. Sam Towler
66. Rob Estes, Josie Bissett's real-life husband
67. Heart attack
68. Celeste
69. Minnesota
70. She'd been diagnosed with AIDS.
71. Columbia University
72. Nancy Donner
73. Suicide at age thirty
74. Irving
75. At a Palm Springs hotel suite where a D&D executive retreat was being held.
76. That she was pregnant—but she later miscarried.
77. Roses covered with black paint
78. A tire iron

SEASON TWO

1. Jo's—because she had a second bedroom and a darkroom for her photography.
2. He whacked his head against a television set.
3. Motorcycle parts
4. Dinner plates
5. Robert Wilson
6. She delivered a hard kick to the groin.
7. A veritable shrine of photographs of Alison spread out on the floor.
8. His laundry
9. Red Sage beer
10. Alison found out that he'd blown his brains out with a gun.
11. Katya was from Russia and wanted to remain in the United States, so they agreed to a marriage of convenience.
12. It blew up when a blowtorch left aflame was knocked over, burning the shop to a crisp.
13. Steve Bryant
14. Arielle
15. She poured a bottle of marinara sauce over his head.

16. Nikki
17. Mara Wilson
18. Computer manufacturing
19. Parker Stevenson
20. At a Russian restaurant
21. Avanti Replicars
22. At the art gallery Joel owned
23. Her lawyer/boyfriend Robert had a restraining order issued, forcing Michael to keep his distance.
24. She smoked a cigarette, perched on his desk.
25. That her mother had abandoned the family when Amanda was eleven.
26. Lauren Etheridge
27. Kristian Alfonso
28. *Days of Our Lives*
29. Carl Canin
30. Stephen Nichols
31. Change the hospital computer records so they wouldn't show Michael's elevated blood alcohol levels.
32. A romantic note from Steve McMillan
33. The F.B.I. warned him he could be considered an accessory if he didn't cooperate with them.
34. Back home to Cleveland
35. Cocaine
36. To Paris, to start a European branch of his computer business
37. Colleen
38. In the confessional of a Catholic church
39. She was homecoming queen at her high school.
40. Reed Carter, an old boyfriend
41. James Wilder
42. Hawaii
43. Her condo was being fumigated
44. Michael
45. That he was a lieutenant in the Navy and they didn't know he was gay.
46. It was in New York City and Alison didn't want to move there with him.
47. Michael mumbled about Matt's changing the hospital computer records regarding Michael's blood alcohol level on the night of the car accident with Kimberly.

48. Gail Strickland
49. He bound and gagged her, and locked her up in the storage compartment.
50. He'd just found out that Billy and Amanda had slept together after he and Amanda had gotten back together, so he punched Billy in the jaw.
51. Jane shoved Sydney into the pool in the wedding gown.
52. Their child—she was pregnant by him when she killed him in self-defense.
53. She told him she didn't want to have sex with him again until after the wedding.
54. $100,000.
55. The grandmother neglected to change the will, so the bequest was to Mr. and Mrs. Michael Mancini.
56. She threw it in the trash.
57. Ted Ryan
58. Dr. Tom Miller
59. He blackmailed Dr. Stanley Levin by showing up for the chief residency announcement with Ingrid, Levin's favorite hooker.
60. She's her mother.
61. Models, Inc.
62. Because she had a long, ugly scar on her head resulting from the brain surgery required after the car accident with Michael.
63. A young model from *Models, Inc.* whom Jo befriended
64. He shoved her down a flight of stairs at the apartment complex when she was pregnant.
65. Hillary Michaels's boyfriend
66. Jungle Jane
67. She removed the "allergic to penicillin" warning label from his patient's chart and he prescribed it, causing the patient to have a seizure.
68. The Australian businessman who wormed his way into Jane's affections and finances.
69. Meredith
70. Tracy Nelson
71. Jane. She showed up for a meeting with Michael, found him, and administered mouth-to-mouth resuscitation.
72. Her father whispering "don't cry" in her ear before the wedding ceremony to Billy.

1. Attempted vehicular manslaughter
2. One of his many enemies, Dr. Stanley Levin
3. She said she was studying at the USC Medical Library.
4. Her Aussie loverboy, Chris
5. Wisconsin
6. He gave information about the magazine to D&D, when Amanda was trying to land *Escapade* as an account.
7. *The Pretty Lady*
8. He used to kiss her on the eyelids to make her laugh.
9. Because she thought it would be best for him, since Reed's parents had sued for custody, and her life was less than settled.
10. He pulled off Kimberly's wig, revealing the red tufts underneath.
11. From her daddy, Palmer
12. Elisabeth
13. Wilshire Memorial
14. The son of one of his college friends
15. She poured a pitcher of water over his head.
16. A black garter belt and bra
17. The Social Services Review committee. Burns objected to what he felt was Kimberly's lack of humanity when it came to dealing with patient concerns.
18. That the apartment's security deposit would be doubled.
19. They went there to stop Jane and Chris from getting hitched. Once that mission was accomplished, they decided to tie the knot themselves.
20. She was a caterer. In fact, she was working a D&D party when she and Alison came to blows and ended up in a major food fight.
21. Michael went off to Las Vegas when he was on call at the hospital.
22. A section of Los Angeles called Los Feliz.
23. His financial interest in Mancini Designs. But Michael being Michael, he pulled a double cross that resulted in Amanda's walking away with nothing.
24. He was a record producer.
25. That she was no longer welcome to be the baby's godmother.
26. Vodka
27. Billy, of course
28. $500,000
29. To Las Vegas

30. At D&D, where Amanda would be sure to find him.
31. Jake. He in turn called Jane, who dragged Michael along.
32. Chicago
33. A mink coat
34. He was a pro football player.
35. Because she was being haunted by nightmares of Bruce and felt that paying the tuition would help make amends.
36. They're both recovering alcoholics.
37. He gave her antibiotics for a flu that contained a drug which tested as if it was the active ingredient in marijuana.
38. Former porn star Traci Lords
39. Meredith hangs her hat in San Francisco.
40. It was none other than Michael Mancini who delivered the bad news.
41. They locked her up in a partially buried box.
42. In Matt's apartment
43. Santa Clarita, California, outside of Los Angeles
44. Because Michael arranged it so that there was a "goof-up" in the reservations.
45. She was the entry coordinator who worked on the "Outstanding Ad Executive" conference. Brooke quickly sized up Alison and started busily networking with her.
46. Glorious Gowns
47. To a small town in Washington State. Jo accompanied him.
48. Made insane, passionate love on her desk.
49. She waited until Billy was in her apartment, and then she pretended to "fall" out of the shower. Naturally, he ran to her rescue and got a good look at her fabulous bod.

50. A paltry $10,000 per year.
51. That she was infertile.
52. Hayley Armstrong
53. Marion Shaw
54. In Miami
55. He was a gardener who had worked for Kimberly's parents when she was a child. She had seen Henry raping her mother and killed him.
56. Daphne Zuniga, who plays Jo
57. He was one of Courtney's victims in the 1995 NBC movie, *Beauty's Revenge*.
58. *Nosferatu*, the 1922 German expressionist vampire film.
59. Rita
60. We'll never tell.

Off-camera, the actors actually get along well together without punching or backstabbing.

Fewer than 20: You belong in the shallow end of the apartment complex pool, kiddo. What have you been doing? Reading books like this one? Get back to the TV and start watching *Melrose*!

20–50: Sounds to us like you identify just a little too much with Jake after a long night behind the bar at Shooters! Better start brushing up on your grasp of meaningless minutiae.

50–100: You're getting there. As you may have surmised from Alison Parker, late nights bent over the books (and the tube) have unexpected rewards, don't they? Go to Shooters and have a beer on us!

100–150: Not bad. . .you obviously have a remote control and know how to wield it. You probably consider Brooke a role model for getting ahead in business.

150–200: My God, you're smart enough to take over for Amanda at D&D! You clearly have your priorities in order. We salute you!!

Lines We *Never* Want to Hear Again!

I'M SORRY.

OH, MY GOD!

WE HAVE TO TALK.

I CAN'T BELIEVE THIS!

YOU'RE CRAZY!

YOU BASTARD!

YOU BITCH!